Kingdom of God, Heritage of Mankind

Kingdom of God, Heritage of Mankind

Unearthing the Mystery from the Creation
of Heavens and Earth

Pindurai Lishandi

RESOURCE *Publications* • Eugene, Oregon

KINGDOM OF GOD, HERITAGE OF MANKIND
Unearthing the Mystery from the Creation of Heavens and Earth

Copyright © 2021 Pindurai Lishandi. All rights reserved. Except for brief quotations in critical publications or reviews, no part of this book may be reproduced in any manner without prior written permission from the publisher. Write: Permissions, Wipf and Stock Publishers, 199 W. 8th Ave., Suite 3, Eugene, OR 97401.

Resource Publications
An Imprint of Wipf and Stock Publishers
199 W. 8th Ave., Suite 3
Eugene, OR 97401

www.wipfandstock.com

PAPERBACK ISBN: 978-1-6667-2906-1
HARDCOVER ISBN: 978-1-6667-2089-1
EBOOK ISBN: 978-1-6667-2090-7

09/08/21

All Scripture quotations, unless otherwise indicated, are taken from the Holy Bible, New International Version®, NIV®. Copyright ©1973, 1978, 1984, 2011 by Biblica, Inc.® Used by permission of Zondervan. All rights reserved worldwide. www.zondervan.com The "NIV" and "New International Version" are trademarks registered in the United States Patent and Trademark Office by Biblica, Inc.®

To my dearly loved wife Rutendo

And our blessed kids
Ngoni, Nyasha, and Nomsa

If God is real, so is the realm in which he exists and everything else that stems from the dominion, the kingdom being no exception.

Contents

Introduction | ix

1 Revelation of the Glory of God | 1
2 The Birth of the Kingdom of Light | 12
3 Image of God in Earthen Vessels | 18
4 God's Sovereign Choice | 31
5 The Promised Land | 38
6 Kingdom of God in the Kingdom of Israel | 46
7 The Church of the Kingdom | 61
8 Expanse of the Eternal Heavenly Kingdom | 74

Introduction

At first I thought it was not specifically written anywhere in the Bible until I found a portion of Scripture with a clue. Enlightenment on one aspect led to the other and together formed a story that I was not keen to forget without passing on, the reason why I decided to write it down.

After many years of being a member of the body of Christ, the persuasive promises of God in the holy Scriptures continued to cultivate in me a deep longing to serve him. But the more I got acquainted with his work, the more questions lingered in my mind to challenge my faith. The foundation of my belief, which I considered to be steadfast, got tested several times amid growing calls for answers to some of life's daunting questions.

Among other things, I needed to be convinced by concise answers on the meaning of the kingdom of God. I often wondered whether the matter was just an abstract notion or something that one can even see and touch. I was very curious to know if it existed in the present or if it will be there in the future. When? Where? Why?

One of the main challenges faced by most people today in their relationship with God is the variety of doctrines and interpretation of Bible Scriptures. This has fragmented believers of the same God to become hostile to fellow believers, much to the laughter of their adversaries, and an obstacle to the mandate of making disciples from all nations.

INTRODUCTION

Confronted with such realities, those who are fond of eternal life continue to search for the truth. But mankind cannot obtain this truth apart from Jesus Christ who is himself the way, the truth, and the life. It therefore implies that gaining that understanding surely revolves around knowing Christ. Unless God, by his grace, reveals his hidden treasures to mankind, many will journey in this life as sailors without a compass; no one knows whether a desired destination would be reached. The possibility of being drifted away by dynamic waves of worldviews and philosophies of this perverse generation becomes inevitable, and the victims wander away from faith at their own peril.

The prudent remain with a quest and unquenched thirst for knowledge. They dissect the word of God day and night to get understanding that dismisses all misconceptions, what a joy when that light comes!

It was that same desire for knowledge which prompted me to carefully study the Scriptures in search for truth about the kingdom of God. I did so with complete reverence to the Word as I believe that all Scripture is God breathed to equip mankind for every good work. This book pursues the kingdom concept in a manner that seeks to bring coherence of the propositions and almost every stone has been turned in the process. The nature of God, mankind, and the realm in which they coexist was penned down as a continuous narrative hinged on Scriptures.

It has an account that is not presumed to be superior to other available theological pieces of writing. Rather, the perspective herein is a humble submission solely from revelation that comes through meditation of Scriptures.

I hope this book will give insight to many as it has to me upon writing.

May glory and honor be given to God, Amen!

1

Revelation of the Glory of God

Salvation of mankind and the subsequent access granted to the kingdom of God are some of the key themes that were more pronounced in the teachings of Jesus Christ. The interpretations of the nature, characteristics, and manifestation of this kingdom vary significantly depending on the perspective from which this subject is approached. Some of the views erroneously eliminate fundamental assertions of Scriptures that were consistent whenever Christ spoke about the kingdom. More often than not, he portrayed this heavenly kingdom as an entity that was somewhat near and within reach, a description that warranted no further search in places far and wide. He emphasized its importance and reality to his disciples, notably so in the period between his resurrection and ascension into heaven.

The Scriptures then say, "And this gospel of the kingdom will be preached in the whole world as a testimony to all nations, and then the end will come" (Matt 24:14, NIV). The question that quickly comes into mind is what does the kingdom of God and gospel of the kingdom entail to merit the value and attention it is given in the Scriptures?

All aspects of the kingdom of God can never be exhausted. However, I believe that the manifestation of God in Jesus Christ, the church that he later established, and the eternal inheritance for the chosen can be construed as the premise of the kingdom concept.

In the context of creation, the inception of the kingdom and the purpose of mankind is evident in the very first three chapters of the book of Genesis. The corresponding details therein form the foundation of the aforementioned presumptions. This may be understood better if the events in these chapters are chronologically analyzed from a kingdom perspective.

These chapters set the scene of what is widely regarded as the beginning. I consider it to be the dawn of features that were formed within particular confines in the expanse of eternity and it does not cover various objects that might have been outside this framework. That which has been created and made known to mankind may just be a minute segment of prior existence in other superior realms that mankind cannot even fathom. Generation upon generation, mankind could not fully comprehend the nature and manifest power of God and as a result various theories arose; some came to be accepted by faith, others by facts and fantasy of science and fiction.

Considering that the words kingdom of God and kingdom of heaven may be used interchangeably, understanding the scope of the kingdom without describing the nature of God and heavenly realms eventually becomes a mountain to climb. These two aspects are related to the kingdom. Apparently, it is most likely that the story of creation in the Bible may also have taken place in those heavenly realms and that view can be gleaned from some veins of the Scriptures. As an entry point to the analysis of the kingdom concept, a quick look into the possible background of creation may be essential.

There is a man who was privileged to converse with the Most High God face-to-face and his experiences are quite intriguing. Because of Moses's immense desire to gain understanding, at one time he drew near a very strange sight of a burning bush that was on fire but not being consumed by the fire. This was a unique and possibly rare event and he heard a voice from God calling him and giving orders from within that bush. The Scriptures record, "God said to Moses, 'I AM WHO I AM. This is what you are to say to the Israelites: I AM has sent me to you'" (Exod 3:14). Moses was hesitant to carry out the mission let alone to continue with the journey with God without knowing full well who exactly "I AM" was. It came to pass that on one fateful day, he gathered his boldness to pursue answers for his far-reaching matters pertaining to the existence of God. The intention was to possibly have all his uncertainties addressed and get further assurance from one last request if granted.

> Then Moses said, "Now show me your Glory." And the Lord said, "I will cause all my goodness to pass in front of you, and I will proclaim my name, the Lord, in your presence. I will have mercy on whom I will have mercy, and I will have compassion on whom I will have compassion." But, God said, "you cannot see my face, for no one may see me and live." Then the Lord said, "There is a place near me where you may stand on a rock. When my glory passes by, I will put you in a cleft in the rock and cover you with my hand until I have passed by. Then I will remove my hand and you will see my back; but my face must not be seen. (Exod 33:18–23)

These Scriptures exhibit an ideal setting for the revelation of the glory of God, such as the one reflected in the story of creation as written in the book of Genesis. The glory that Moses wanted to see was a superior dimension of the nature of God and he expected it to be brought forth in a measure that he had never experienced before. I believe that this glory of God may be referred to as the goodness, presence, or fullness of God that exhibits the complete sovereign nature and power of God.

I suppose it might not be possible for mankind to see this nature of God from a physical location. From that suggestion, therefore, the setting given by the Scriptures for the unveiling of the glory of God to Moses may be figurative. Its consequent manifestation may have happened in the form of a revelation from the heavenly realms where this dimension of God can be revealed.

One great question from Moses led to a series of instructions concerning the revelation of the glory of God, the actual encounter for which the Scriptures do not plainly provide. But is the Bible completely silent on that? I do not believe so. There are a couple of clues that may help in understating the encounter Moses had in the revelation of the glory of God.

The Scriptures say that at one time when Jesus Christ was with his disciples, he prayed for quite a number of things including those people who will later believe in him. He said, "Father, I want those you have given me to be with me where I am, and to see my glory, the glory you have given me because you loved me before the creation of the world" (John 17:24). When Jesus Christ made this prayer, he was physically surrounded by his disciples. I do not think that every believer is meant to be at that very same physical location to see his glory. However, the implication of his words may mean that he longed for his believers to be with him in the realm where he was when he prayed. That location is an expanse from where his glory can be seen and is separate from the place where he was physically located. That realm could be the same as the one where Moses might have been taken to see the glory of God.

Prior to the day Jesus Christ made this prayer, the Scriptures say that he asked his disciples if they knew who he was. It was Simon who, upon having a revelation from God, proclaimed that Jesus was the Christ and Son of the living God. Upon this declaration, Jesus then replied and said to him, "And I tell you that you are Peter, and on this rock I will build my church, and the gates of Hades will not overcome it" (Matt 16:18).

I believe that the rock referred to in that scenario may have meant a solid and firm foundation of revelation through which mankind can get to receive information from God. It is most likely then that the rock where Moses was placed might symbolize the revelation he was to be given in order to witness the glory of God.

The Scriptures also say that at one time Paul the apostle was taken into a realm which the word of God refers to as a heavenly realm. He could not even tell whether he got into such a realm in body or out of the body. In most cases, the things that happen in such a realm can only be perceived while one is still in that realm as they do not follow the norms of the physical realm. The once vivid experiences from that realm slowly fade away as the memories gradually become meaningless to the mind.

The events in such realms occur in an infinite space without passage of the time that we know. The objects of those realms are real, with endless manifestation possibilities that are only limited by the capacity of the beholder. I believe when a person goes to sleep and has a dream, it all happens in one such kind of realm. In a dream, a person can travel for thousands of miles and do many things over a period that may span a couple of hours or days in that dream, yet it will all be happening in a few seconds that the person dozes off.

Thus, Moses was probably given access to one of the realms of the Most High, a heavenly realm where God would determine the extent of the glory he would reveal. He was already made aware of the fact that he would not see God's face in the revelation of the glory but only see God's back. But does God have a human form that has a face and back? Surely not; God is not a man. I believe the reference to the face and back in the context of that revelation may allude to stages in the existence of God. Perhaps not seeing God's face, but rather his back, may imply that Moses was not able to see the approach of God to the scene but his exit. This has been illustrated by Moses being covered by the hand of God and put in a cleft. From that perspective of the manifestation of the glory of God, Moses in the revelation did not even see where God came from but rather where he was heading, his purpose, and plan. To this day, mankind cannot tell the origins of God and I will not even attempt to tackle that subject. It is a mystery. Maybe God does not even have to come from somewhere to become, for he already was what he is and will be.

In light of that background, the point from which Moses began to witness the glory of God marked the genesis of the revelation to him.

Many people consider Moses to be the probable writer of the book of Genesis. Obviously he was not physically present to witness creation. However, I am convinced that the Scriptures from the initial chapters of the book of Genesis contain records that, if harmonized, are suggestive of the glory of God that he requested to see. They seem to be a narrative of events initially seen as a revelation and then later passed on as a story that was immortalized in writing. If that is the case, then the glory that Moses saw was perhaps a series of successive events that displayed God's splendor both discretely and collectively.

Several aspects of the existence of God are introduced at creation and they include the sovereign being of the Godhead, the kingdom of his glory, and the man who carried his image.

The Bible categorically states, "In the beginning God created the heavens and the earth. Now the earth was formless and empty, darkness was all over the surface of the deep, and the Spirit of God was hovering over the waters" (Gen 1:1–2).

Evidently, even in that beginning, there were factors already in existence before creation commenced. God was there, so was the Spirit of God who was seen hovering over the waters. But where was Jesus Christ and what was his relationship to the Spirit of God? It may be helpful to take a step-by-step approach into this matter and break down the basic things that are being highlighted by this Scripture.

There is a common term used by believers today, which I think has resulted in differences on how the nature of God is depicted. The word "Trinity" has found its way to be accepted as the best way of describing the triune nature of God, but not without dispute. From the concept of Trinity: God the Father, the Spirit of God, and Jesus Christ are seen as three equal and separate infinite entities of but one God. As much as I believe that these supernatural beings are equal and infinite, I am more of the opinion that since they are spiritual beings, they cannot be enumerated and are therefore inseparable but omnipresent. I consider the names to be separate but not the beings themselves.

This nature of God is not easy to understand. The Scriptures say, "No one has ever seen God, but the one and only Son, who is himself God and in closest relationship with the Father, has made him known" (John 1:18). I take this to be a supreme declaration that Christ was apparently there at creation as he is God. The Scriptures say that at one time upon being asked about the greatest commandment, Jesus said, "'The most important one,' answered Jesus, 'is this: Hear, O Israel: The Lord our God, the Lord is one'" (Mark 12:29).

This points to the fact that the nature of God in his entirety is reflected as one and no other apart from him. On another instance Jesus told the Jews who were around him that "I and the Father are one" (John 10:30). I consider these to be absolute statements that are fundamental in understanding the nature of God. Another passage of Scripture says, "For God was pleased to have all his fullness dwell in Him" (Col 1:19). This could be the reason why Jesus Christ rebuked one of his disciples for lack of the understanding that he was indeed God. The Scriptures have a record:

> Philip said, "Lord, show us the Father and that will be enough for us." Jesus answered: "Don't you know me, Philip, even after I have been among you such a long time? Anyone who has seen me has seen the Father. How can you say, 'Show us the Father'? Don't you believe that I am in the Father, and that the Father is in me? The words I say to you I do not speak on my own authority. Rather, it is the Father, living in me, who is doing his work. (John 14:8–10)

From this understanding, I believe there is but one God whose attributes manifest in various forms and mankind has been privileged to witness these characteristics in Jesus Christ and Holy Spirit who in turn is also God. Yes, it may be confusing but the evidence from the word of God on these matters is substantial.

The Scriptures have an account that Peter the apostle of Jesus Christ at one time reminded believers by saying, "But just as he who called you is holy, so be holy in all you do; for it is written: 'Be holy, because I am holy'" (1 Pet 1:15–16). From this Scripture it is clear that God is holy. Not only that, in one of the famous stories in the Bible Jesus also said to a Samaritan woman, "God is spirit, and his worshipers must worship in the Spirit and in truth" (John 4:24). These two Scriptures mean that the same God who is holy is also spirit. This could be the most basic way of illustrating that if God is holy and spirit it implies that he is the Holy Spirit, the Spirit of God that manifested and hovered over the waters at creation.

When the coming of Jesus Christ was foretold, the Scriptures say that "The virgin will conceive and give birth to a son, and they will call him Immanuel" (which means "God with us") (Matt 1:23). Thus, Jesus Christ was to be the manifestation of God in human form. The Scriptures also say, "In your relationships with one another, have the same mindset as Christ Jesus: Who, being in very nature God, did not consider equality with God something to be used to his own advantage; rather, he made himself nothing by taking the very nature of a servant, being made in human likeness" (Phil 2:5–7).

The evidence of the Scriptures incline more to Jesus Christ being God than anything else, and therefore I believe that at creation he was part of the Godhead. The word of God says,

> For in Him all things were created: things in heaven and on earth, visible and invisible, whether thrones or powers or rulers or authorities; all things have been created for him and through him. He is before all things and in Him all things hold together. (Col 1:16–17)

These affirmations do not make Jesus Christ to be any less than God, let alone be regarded discretely as the power of the words that proceeded from the mouth of God at creation.

This omnipresent nature of God helps to remove quite a number of obstacles in the path of grasping the revelation of the glory of God that was written down in the account of creation.

There is hardly any indication as to how God created the heavens and the earth, whether words were used or not. The recorded reference to God's very first words came after the heavens and earth were created. Yet the Scriptures say,

> In the beginning was the Word, and the Word was with God, and the Word was God. Through him all things were made; without Him nothing was made that has been made. The Word became flesh and made his dwelling among us. We have seen his glory, the glory of the one and only Son, who came from the Father, full of grace and truth. (John 1:1–3, 14)

I am of the opinion that as much as the Word was the manifestation of Jesus Christ, the spoken words at creation were driven by the power of the purpose that prompted creation. In the beginning was that purpose with God, it had authority to create all things out of nothing and existed outside the boundaries of the words that came forth from the mouth of God.

In order to get a better appreciation of the story of creation, further categories would need to be outlined. There are two distinct realms that I believe to have been created in the beginning: one physical and the other non-physical. I take the non-physical realms to be the heavens, located in the heavenly realms. They have the nature of heaven, a realm where God has his throne. These were superior realms that mankind cannot see by the physical eye but elements thereof have the power to sustain and dominate the objects in the physical realm. Both the Spirit of God and the spirit of darkness reside in those realms, hence the name "spiritual realms."

On the other hand, the physical realm is all that mankind can touch and see, far and wide: the waters, the dry ground, and the vast other elements of the universe.

So after God created the heavens and the earth, it is recorded that darkness covered the surface of the deep. There is no mention as well as to where this darkness came from. I believe that it was not a physical darkness, as no physical light had been created, absence of which can cause physical darkness. I would like to think that this was a form of darkness in the heavenly realms; the ultimate spiritual power of evil that had been present even before creation of the heavens and earth. I believe that this power of darkness goes far beyond the devil and it may be the very source of all kinds of evil. It could be this power that caused the mind of one of God's angels to become conceited and want to be like God, which is why it was later cast down onto earth as Satan, the angel of darkness.

I therefore consider the deep to be a source or realm of a particular nature and in this case, the heavenly realm. The Scriptures say that at one time Jesus Christ taught multitudes from a boat where Simon was seated, listening. "When he had finished speaking, he said to Simon, 'Put out into deep water, and let down the nets for a catch'" (Luke 5:4). Maybe the power of the words from Christ when he taught the multitudes made Simon believe in Christ's authority. The instruction that was given to Simon had little to do with the physical depth of the water or a possible location in the sea. The deep was probably the realm where the words that Simon later acknowledged and acted upon came from.

I believe that at creation the power of darkness thus covered the periphery of the realm where the spirits dwell, the heavenly realms. It follows then that the Spirit of God and the power of darkness initially took charge of different realms at creation and their positions were very strategic.

The reasons can be understood from the purpose and plan that made God commence creation in the first place. It is unlikely that God would have started creation without having a goal in the co-existence of multiple objects of the physical and heavenly realms. Surely God had a purpose, that which was also embraced by his words. As it is to mankind that life without fulfilling a purpose is futile, so would creation have become if there was no purpose.

The Scriptures say that one day Satan appeared when the angels came to present themselves before the LORD. This gives me an impression that the evil one can somehow gain information on the purpose and plan of God, hence the early positioning in the heavenly realms. If the evil one was well placed, so then was the Spirit of God when it hovered over the waters of a formless and empty physical realm.

The purpose of God is always set out from start to finish before it is executed. As God is the alpha and the omega, he does not become the omega at a later stage after being the alpha but he is the alpha at a time when he is the omega. The Scriptures say that he makes known the end from the beginning and his purpose will stand and he accomplishes all that he pleases. God purposes every word that proceeds forth from his mouth that it does not return to him without achieving the result for which it was sent. Definitely God had a vivid plan with the heavens and the earth, a purpose that the power of darkness was attempting to thwart.

At the center of the ultimate plan of God was the establishment of his kingdom and eternal life for mankind to whom that kingdom was going to be given as inheritance. If it was a matter of priority, then the creation of that kingdom was imminent after the establishment of the heavens and the earth. But what exactly was that kingdom?

2

The Birth of the Kingdom of Light

The creation of heavens and earth laid the foundation for everything else that followed in the story of creation. I would like to believe that when God called things into existence thereafter, some of the events manifested in the heavenly realms and others in the physical realm.

The Scriptures say, "And God said, 'Let there be light,' and there was light" (Gen 1:3). I am of the understanding that this light may not have been a physical light in the form of the light that comes from the sun or any other physical source. In any case, at this particular stage in the order of creation the sun had not been created as well.

This light at creation must have manifested in the heavenly realms where the power of darkness was located and I consider that light to be a symbol of the pre-incarnation of Jesus Christ. Inherent that light was the power of God and it marked the establishment of the first aspect of the kingdom of God in the heavenly realms; the eternal heavenly dwelling.

There are multiple references to this light in the Scriptures. To begin with, the Scriptures say, "When Jesus spoke again to the people, he said, 'I am the light of the world. Whoever follows me will never walk in darkness, but will have the light of life'" (John 8:12). Christ declared that he was the light. If that was the case then the exhibition of the light in an expanse with the power of darkness was possibly a sign of his taking over of dominion in that space of the heavenly realms.

The word of God also has a record that when Paul the apostle encouraged believers to live a life that pleases God, he said to them,

> And giving joyful thanks to the Father, who has qualified you to share in the inheritance of his holy people in the kingdom of light. For he has rescued us from the dominion of darkness and brought us into the kingdom of the Son he loves, in whom we have redemption, the forgiveness of sins. (Col 1:12–14)

I suppose Paul was pointing to the kingdom of God in the heavenly realms, a kingdom established by Christ who is the light and the fullness of God. At some stage in ministry, John the disciple of Jesus Christ had a revelation of the Holy City, the New Jerusalem. The Scriptures say, "The city does not need the sun or the moon to shine on it, for the glory of God gives it light, and the Lamb is its lamp" (Rev 21:23). This is another example where Christ, the Lamb of God, is shown as possessing and giving out the light. John also strengthened believers and confidently said, "This is the message that we heard from Him and declare to you: God is light, in him there is no darkness at all" (1John 1:5).

The light at creation was a manifestation of the Godhead in an expanse of the heavenly realms where the power of darkness was located. Thus, when God said "Let there be light," he was positioning his eternal kingdom in the heavenly realms for his chosen—ready to be fashioned for his pleasure.

The manifest light of God conquered amid all the possible resistance from the power of darkness. That light was eternal, and so was the kingdom that was established. The word of God figuratively points to Christ and his victory over the darkness in the heavenly realms when it says, "In him was life, and that life was the light of all mankind. The light shines in the darkness, and the darkness has not overcome it" (John 1:4–5).

Mankind still wage a war with the evil one to this day because of the victory that the light had over darkness. The Scriptures say, "For our struggle is not against flesh and blood, but against the rulers, against the authorities, against the powers of this dark world and against the spiritual forces of evil in the heavenly realms" (Eph 6:12). I presume that the powers of this dark world are a product of the powers of darkness.

So after the creation of the kingdom of light, God went on to separate the light from the darkness. I believe that God separated his kingdom from the kingdom of darkness in the heavenly realms but possibly left them in close proximity. The Scriptures say, "God called the light 'day,' and the darkness he called 'night.' And there was evening, and there was morning—the first day" (Gen 1:5). It has never been easy to quantify the period in which events happen in the heavenly realms. The sun had not yet been created to measure time in the order of hours and minutes that add up to become days of the physical realm. Perhaps the correlation between the light that was "day" and "the first day" of creation could be that they were reminiscent of the other and this was no coincidence.

If the light did not manifest in the physical realm, the first day may not have been a span of hours. Rather, it may be taken to be a mark of the initial discrete and complete show of the glory of God.

At one time Jesus Christ said to the people, "Your father Abraham rejoiced at the thought of seeing my day, he saw it and was glad" (John 8:56). Which day was this and when did Abraham see it? Probably the implication of "day" may not be a physical one, as Abraham died long before the coming of Jesus Christ. The Scriptures say that at some stage Abraham met Melchizedek, the king of Salem and priest of God Most High, he was blessed and he gave him a tenth of everything he had.

This Melchizedek was king of Salem and priest of God Most High. He met Abraham returning from the defeat of the kings and blessed him, and Abraham gave him a tenth of everything. First, the name Melchizedek means "king of righteousness"; then also, "king of Salem" means "king of peace." Without father or mother, without genealogy, without beginning of days or end of life, resembling the Son of God, he remains a priest forever. (Heb 7:1–3)

I believe that Melchizedek may be a typology of Christ and probably the "day" that Abraham saw, the "day" that was the light of God at creation. The Scriptures say, "You are children of the light and children of the day. We do not belong to the night or to the darkness" (1 Thess 5:5). This further shows that the "day" at creation may have been the glory of God in Jesus Christ. Likewise, the night at creation typified the power of the evil one.

However, even if the day at creation is considered to be a measure of a period of time in the physical realm, the Scriptures say, "But do not forget this one thing, dear friends: With the Lord a day is like a thousand years, and a thousand years are like a day" (2 Peter 3:8). This may mean that the day at creation may also be a span of time different from the contemporary standard measure. However, this does not in any way disqualify God's ability to have created everything in the twinkling of an eye or in a span of twenty-four hours as in the common physical day. Whichever way the day is interpreted, with God nothing is impossible.

After the manifestation of the kingdom of light in the heavenly realms, God bestowed onto it a greatest value by virtue of purpose but had to ensure that mankind could comprehend that value and significance.

It is at that stage that God commenced creating objects in the physical realm where the Holy Spirit hovered over the waters. I believe that God deliberately began to create objects in the physical realm that resembled aspects of the heavenly realm so as to enhance mankind's understanding of the latter. This has been consistent even in the teachings of Jesus Christ who constantly used parables that were earthly stories with heavenly meanings. Similarly, the Scriptures also personify God even though he is Spirit. Reference is made to his hands, eyes, face, and ears, to mention but a few things. Perhaps God knew that his nature and purpose could not be fully understood from the wisdom of mankind, hence the use of objects that could be easily perceived by the mind.

The models created on earth were meant, among other reasons, to remind mankind of many aspects of the kingdom of God. The physical realm was therefore adorned with features that were a shadow of the heavenly kingdom so that through them mankind would be able to relate with the spiritual realms. So God created the sky to separate the water above from the water below to form a distinct gap between the once single expanse of water. The water under the sky was gathered to form seas and possibly rivers, tributaries and distributaries and dry ground appeared as a landmass from the water. This is the area that was once watched over by the Spirit of God. The dry ground that appeared was to be the dwelling place for the physical man for a set period of time and the kingdom of the light was reserved for the spirit of mankind in eternity.

Later on, vegetation, seed-bearing plants, and trees were also created. Most of the creation on earth was seen by John as features in the revelation of the New Jerusalem which came out of the heavenly realms. The Scriptures say,

> Then the angel showed me the river of the water of life, as clear as crystal, flowing from the throne of God and of the Lamb down the middle of the great street of the city. On each side of the river stood the tree of life, bearing twelve crops of fruit, yielding its fruit every month. And the leaves of the tree are for the healing of the nations. (Rev 22:1–2)

God went on to create lights in the vault of the sky to give light to the physical realm, to separate day from night, and to govern the day and the night. The greater light for the day was the sun and the lesser light for the night was the moon. This separation of the day from the night in the physical realm resembled the separation of the "day" and "night" in the establishment of the kingdom of light in the heavenly realms. The existence of the two separate kingdoms in the heavenly realms became evident on earth, with the physical light being supreme over darkness in the same way the light of God reigned over the power of darkness in the heavenly realms.

Not only were the sun and moon meant give remembrance of the kingdom of God, they were also meant to serve as signs to mark sacred times and days and years in the physical realm. Time on earth became wholly encompassed within the everlasting. The physical light was used to measure time in the order of days the same way in Christ, the "day," there is the complete measure of the infinite time-eternal life. Even to this present day reference to Christ in the counting of years is unmistakable, with BC meaning 'Before Christ' and AD being 'In the year of our Lord.'

Further in the story of creation, God created living creatures: some that live in water, those that fly in the air, and all the wild animals and livestock. All these creations gave glory to God and he pronounced a blessing of fruitfulness and multiplication on them.

But mankind was yet to be created. The one for whom the kingdom was reserved as an inheritance in the fullness of time was yet to come into being. Why then was mankind chosen among all creation to inherit the kingdom? Even the Psalmist in the Scriptures wondered and asked God, "What is mankind that you are mindful of them, human beings that you care for them" (Ps 8:4).

3

Image of God in Earthen Vessels

The record of the creation of mankind is given in separate chapters of the Scriptures in the book of Genesis, one preceding the other. However, I believe that a combination of the facts in those chapters present a continuous narrative of the same event. The first of those two chapters gives more of what I consider to be a summary of the process, which then got elaborated in the later chapter.

For all the other creation before mankind, God just spoke things into being and they became; the Scriptures did not outline the process involved. The constituent elements used in the creation of those objects are not obvious and remain a mystery. The Scriptures say, "By faith we understand that the universe was made at God's command so that what is seen was not made out of what was visible" (Heb 11:3). Perhaps some invisible attributes were used. But when it came to the creation of mankind, finer details were provided to highlight some key features of the outcome. I guess this was provided for mankind to be able to have an appreciation of the coexistence of spiritual and physical factors.

At the stage when God created mankind, the kingdom of light had already been established in the heavenly realms. The land in the physical realm had also produced vegetation—trees and seed-bearing plants. However, in the passage where the actual steps of the creation of mankind are outlined, the Scriptures say, "Now no shrub had yet appeared on the earth and no plant had yet sprung up, for the Lord God had not sent rain on the earth and there was no one to work the ground, but streams came up from the earth and watered the whole surface of the ground" (Gen 2:5–6). My perception is that as much as God had given every plant a unique seed, the blessing for the land to be productive and fruitful was yet to come through the creation of mankind. And for that reason, no seed had produced even a tender shoot from the ground before mankind was created. The Scriptures have a record:

> Then God said, "Let us make mankind in our image, in our likeness, so that they may rule over the fish in the sea and the birds in the sky, over the livestock and all the wild animals, and over all the creatures that move along the ground." (Gen 1:26)

Mankind was to be given dominion over almost everything in the physical realm and this dominance was to come as an inherent ability at his disposal. All the exploits of mankind from the use of this dominion was meant to give glory to God.

But who was God speaking to when he said "Let us make man in our image"?

God is Spirit. He had already manifested as the Holy Spirit that hovered over the waters. God had also revealed himself as the light, Jesus Christ, in establishing his kingdom in the heavenly realms. In the context of creation, I believe that a testimony of the Godhead in creating mankind may be taken to be a form of a conversation. Apart from that, I suppose there were other heavenly beings that were already in existence before mankind was created.

The Scriptures have a record of a dialogue between God and a man called Job. At one particular instance, God posed a question to Job and said,

> Where were you when I laid the earth's foundation? Tell me if you understand. Who marked off its dimensions? Surely you know! Who stretched a measuring line across

it? On what where its footings set, or who laid its cornerstone—while the morning stars sang together and all the angels shouted for joy? (Job 38:4–7)

This may mean that angels and other heavenly hosts may have been there before mankind was created. Whichever case it may be, God wanted to create mankind to have his resemblance, not in the outward appearance but rather in the inward adornment. As the image of an object bears the characteristics of that object, therefore mankind was to reflect the nature of God who is Spirit by having that likeness and carrying a spirit that had the nature of God. And so in the fullness of time, God took dust from the earth in the physical realm and framed the body of man; the earth from which the Holy Spirit probably hovered over to protect for such a noble use. By making use of the dust from the earth to form a body, I believe God also wanted mankind to bear the likeness of both the spiritual and the physical as he was going to simultaneously belong to both realms.

The body that was created from the dust of the earth existed for an undetermined period before it was made alive. After that, God then took a characteristic that resembled his nature, a life giving spirit, and breathed that through the nostrils of the body and the man became a living being. It is likely that some aspects of the fullness of God were withheld on the spirit that was given to the body. Perhaps God knew that those attributes were complex to be managed by mankind while the image of God was still in the body of dust. For instance, the man God created did not primarily have the same knowledge of good and evil that God had. Thus, mankind was created with an adaptation to his existence in the physical realm.

The spirit inside mankind appealed to God who is Spirit. The communion that God had with mankind from then on was through the spirit of man, the same spirit that was intended to remind him of the existence of the heavenly kingdom. The hub of the spirit became the soul of mankind and the mind a nucleus of the flesh.

The spirit inside man and the flesh that embodied it were to coexist for a period set by God, with the soul being so pronounced and active to overshadow the functions of the mind.

In having the first man Adam to carry the forms of these two distinct realms, God wanted to make mankind to belong to each realm with full rights as a subject and citizen of each kingdom.

After mankind was created the Scriptures say, "God blessed them and said to them, 'Be fruitful and increase in number; fill the earth and subdue it. Rule over the fish in the sea and the birds in the sky and over every living creature that moves on the ground'" (Gen 1:28).

I believe that this blessing was bestowed on the body of dust, the physical nature of man. The spirit inside man can be considered to have been blessed by default since it was the image of God. Perhaps when God pronounced that blessing on mankind, everything that had the likeness of the physical nature of man also received the blessing, including the land from which dust was taken to form the body of mankind.

The land that had not produced any fruit thus became fruitful and that blessing was like showers of rain sent down by God in season.

This was the sixth time God exhibited the goodness of what he had made out of the power of his purpose. The heavens and the earth were all created in their vast array. And upon completion of all his work of creating, God rested.

After the creation of mankind, there was no evening and there was no morning, which could be an indication that mankind was left in the presence of the power of the light, the expanse of the "day." I believe God wanted mankind to have an appreciation of that period of rest and its significance in the heavenly realms. God later commanded mankind to observe that rest on a particular day in the physical realm as a Sabbath. The day of rest under the light from the sun in the physical realm pointed to the eternal life of the kingdom of God which is a rest in the light who is Jesus Christ. The Scriptures say,

> Therefore do not let anyone judge you by what you eat or drink, or with regard to a religious festival, a New Moon celebration or a Sabbath day. These are a shadow of the things that were to come; the reality, however, is found in Christ. (Col 2:16–17)

Thus, the Sabbath rest carried a spiritual connotation. Another passage of Scripture says, "There remains, then, a Sabbath-rest for the people of God; for anyone who enters God's rest also rests from their works, just as God did from his" (Heb 4:9–10). I believe that this is not only in observance of one physical day without manual work but also the acceptance of the everlasting rest that comes when mankind retires from the work of the flesh and surrenders to the work of his Spirit. The word of God says, "Being confident of this, that he who began a good work in you will carry it on to completion until the day of Christ Jesus" (Phil 1:6). And also another Scripture says, "For it is God who works in you to will and to act in order to fulfill his good purpose" (Phil 2:13). Jesus Christ is the one who ushers people into that rest and in him is the rest. At creation, God's rest was the exhibition of the plan of eternal life for mankind as the future of mankind had already been set and sealed.

Even without knowledge of good and bad, Adam was given wisdom to live with, a kind of wisdom that enabled him to fellowship and converse with God and interact with nature without any fear. I suppose Adam, with the wisdom he had, could attest to almost everything that he accomplished after he became a living being and that information may have been passed on from generation to generation.

God had the responsibility of making Adam understand that he had been chosen among all creation to inherit the purposed heavenly kingdom. So God planted a garden in the east, in Eden, and there he put the man he had formed.

The Scriptures say,

> The Lord God made all kinds of trees grow out of the ground, trees that were pleasing to the eye and were good for food. In the middle of the garden were the tree of life and the tree of the knowledge of good and evil. The Lord God took the man and put him in the garden of Eden to work it and take care of it. And the Lord God commanded the man, "You are free to eat from any tree in the garden; but you must not eat from the tree of the knowledge of good and evil, for when you eat from it you will certainly die. (Gen 2:9, 15–17)

I believe this was a great step in God's purpose to bring to the attention of Adam the idea of the heavenly kingdom. God put the two trees in the garden, which I believe were not distinct from all the other trees in Eden in their physical nature but were made sacred by the virtue of the their purpose in the garden. There were consequences in Adam eating the fruits from these trees; the tree of life in Eden was meant to give eternal life and the tree of the knowledge of good and evil resulting in death. The disobedience of the statutes of God is sin and it is caused by the powers from the kingdom of darkness.

So in essence, the trees can be figuratively considered to be two kingdoms placed by God before Adam, one of life and the other of death. I would like to think that the fruits from the tree of life represented the life that came from the kingdom of the light. On the other hand, the fruits from the tree of the knowledge of good and evil denoted the death that would result from disobedience to God's commands. One kingdom had eternal life for the spirit of man, and the other was without, lack of which was the death of the spirit.

In seeing these trees every single day, Adam was supposed to be reminded of the life and death that was set for his spirit and he had to make a choice. Thus, two distinct kingdoms were placed side by side in the garden of Eden in the form of these trees, the same way the kingdom of light existed alongside the kingdom of darkness in the heavenly realms.

If Adam is considered to have had equal access to both trees, so are the choices of mankind even today. The Scriptures say,

> This day I call the heavens and the earth as witnesses against you that I have set before you life and death, blessings and curses. Now choose life, so that you and your children may live. (Deut 30:19)

Adam had a chance to make a choice to belong to any of the kingdoms set before him. The eating was as commitment to belong to the kingdom partaken of its fruits.

The Scriptures say,

> Now what I am commanding you today is not too difficult for you or beyond your reach. It is not up in heaven, so that you have to ask, who will ascend into heaven to get it and proclaim it to us so we may obey it? Nor is it beyond the sea, so that you have to ask, who will cross the sea to get it and proclaim it to us so we may obey it? No, the word is very near you; it is in your mouth and in your heart so you may obey it. See, I set before you today life and prosperity, death and destruction. (Deut 30:11–15)

So the inheritance of eternal life of the kingdom was at Adam's disposal, right within arm's reach. God had purposed Adam to have eternal life for his spirit and that was the intended plan for all generations through him. The Scriptures say, "For God so loved the world that he gave his one and only Son, that whoever believes in him would not die but have eternal life" (John 3:16). The eternal life that was once meant to come from Adam's obedience then later came through Jesus Christ, the second Adam.

The clear instructions given to Adam regarding the two trees also gave the message that God did not want mankind to belong to both kingdoms but only choose to be in one and not the other. And not only that, mankind was not at any time intended to learn about the heavenly kingdom from anyone else apart from God. This is a challenge even in our modern days, mankind tend to pay attention to manifestations from the spirit of darkness professing about the knowledge of God. I believe that the things of God are meant to be made known by the Spirit of God.

However, the devil was crafty and cunning, knowing full well the destiny of mankind and how the choices set before him were a matter of life or death for the spirit. I believe that since the power of darkness had not prevailed in the establishment of the kingdom of the light in the heavenly realms, the tree of life was a reminder of the victories of God. So the devil plotted a plan to distract mankind and possibly get rid of the opportunity for eternal life. From an informed position, the devil negotiated with mankind and presented twisted truth blended with lies in deceit.

The Scriptures say that the devil is very cunning. Jesus at one time said to the Jews, "You belong to your father, the devil, and you want to carry out your father's desires. He was a murderer from the beginning, not holding to the truth, for there is no truth in him. When he lies, he speaks his native language, for he is a liar and the father of lies" (John 8:44).

Surely, the tree of knowledge of good and evil was meant to open the eyes of mankind and become like God, knowing good and bad. I believe regardless of how true the testimony was, because it had come from the evil one it should not have been entertained or obeyed. The Scriptures say that Paul the apostle had to rebuke a spirit from a fortune teller even if the spirit was confessing the truth. There is a record that says,

> She followed Paul and the rest of us, shouting, "These men are servants of the Most High God, who are telling you the way to be saved." She kept this up for many days. Finally Paul became so annoyed that he turned around and said to the spirit, "In the name of Jesus Christ I command you to come out of her!" At that moment the spirit left her. (Acts 16:17–18)

I believe death was not the consequence of having the knowledge of good and bad. God had that knowledge but has eternal life. Deliberately, the devil did not tell mankind that the death would come from the act of disobedience to God's command. This could be the reason why even the mere touching of the forbidden tree may have resulted in death without even partaking of the fruit. Jesus Christ said in the Scriptures, "But I tell you that anyone who looks at a woman lustfully has already committed adultery with her in his heart" (Matt 5:28). Sin therefore precedes the act.

Mankind was on the brink of losing eternal life by touching the forbidden tree let alone eating its fruit. Sadly, man chose to accept guidance from the devil and by so doing lost his inheritance of the Kingdom and that was the death of his spirit. Adam lost the eternal life for the spirit by eating the fruits from the forbidden tree. Perhaps that life would have possibly been retained by access to the tree of life. This concept could be the same as when a person backslides after gaining salvation from Jesus Christ; repentance and coming back to God is a way of regaining eternal life.

Without the knowledge of good and bad, Adam had dominion in the physical realm. He could command animals to come to him and give them identity without any fear and knowledge of danger. He had no lack for his needs, his spirit dominated his flesh and canal mind, he lived for God and was on course heading for the set destiny of inheriting the heavenly kingdom.

However, after Adam ate the fruit his eyes were suddenly opened and the first thing that came to him was a sense of fear, shame, and nakedness. That was part of the knowledge he had now gained. He had always been physically naked from creation and he never knew from looking with his eyes that he was naked. That lack of knowledge was like a cover to his eyes. Perhaps that it was that cover for his nakedness which got removed by the knowledge that came from his disobedience. That which was removed for man to see his nakedness was a symbol of the lost dominance of the soul of mankind over the mind, the spirit over the flesh.

I do not think that Adam was initially created with immortality of his physical body though. The same way people who believe in Jesus Christ still die physically even after receiving eternal life for their spirit, possibly Adam could still have died regardless of his sin. Perhaps there was a predestination of life and death for his physical form and also eternal life and death of his spirit. For the Scriptures say, "From one man he made all nations, that they should inhabit the whole earth; and he marked out their appointed times in history and the boundaries of their land. God did this so that they would seek him and perhaps reach out for him and find him, though he is not far from any one of us" (Acts 17:26–27).

When mankind realized that he was naked, he sewed the leaves of a fig tree and made a cover for himself and hid from God among the trees in the garden. In other words, Adam realized that evil had come into him after being enticed by the devil; he understood that God was good and opposed to all evil. Evidently, Adam had chosen to belong to a kingdom whose demands were very challenging. A kingdom that called for responsibility and accountability for every action and he had no permanent solutions for the imminent problems that awaited him.

Assuming that God used to meet with Adam at a particular place on every visitation in the garden of Eden, on one fateful day Adam was absent. His soul did not prompt him to avail himself before God but rather his mind led him to move away from him.

However, because God longed for the fellowship he had with the soul of the man he had created, he was filled with compassion and extended an invite. The word of God says, "But the Lord God called to the man, 'Where are you?'" (Gen 3:9). Figuratively, God was searching for his spirit in Adam that was now hardly seen for it had dwindled, became dormant and overshadowed by the flesh.

God was angry with mankind for the negligence. Instead of taking heed of his instructions, mankind had paid attention to the guidance and direction of the devil. God was not pleased with the man he had created. However, God did not curse Adam who had sinned but rather cursed the ground from which he had formed mankind. Perhaps God could not directly curse that which he had already blessed. The curse made to the ground was meant to disadvantage and punish man the same way the blessing bestowed on him prior also benefited the ground from which he was formed.

The image of God inside of man from then on dwelled in a body made from the ground that was cursed and the dominion of the spirit of mankind was compromised. Fear, pain, and sorrow became his portion and Adam started to fend for himself and this became the norm for all mankind. The fruitfulness that initially came through as a blessing was now a result obtained through hard work, effort, and pain.

Adam did not ask for forgiveness for his wrongdoing; his spirit was overtaken by pride and fear. The spirit inside man struggled with the flesh that housed it and continued to yearn for spiritual things in the heavenly kingdom from a distance at a time when the flesh grew interest of pursuing the pleasures of the physical kingdom. The Scriptures say, "For the flesh desires what is contrary to the Spirit, and the Spirit contrary to the flesh. They are in conflict to each other so that you do not do whatever you want" (Gal 5:17).

This marked the start of labor in the life of man in the kingdom to which he had chosen for himself. For the first time the spirit inside of man suffered from the loss of communion with God because of the sin from disobedience. But God was filled with compassion and mercy and brought a better solution to the man who was covered with fig leaves; an act that showed the righteousness that comes from God as opposed to self-righteousness. God made a garment of skin and gave it to man to replace the fig leaves. Blood had to be spilled from the death of an animal in order to cover Adam's shame. This sincere and surpassing act of love from God to man was meant to provoke man's heart to accept reconciliation with his maker.

Though the nakedness was covered, the sin remained because Adam had not repented. God had to find another way of making man understand that disobedience of God's statute constituted sin and it is why mankind had lost the inheritance of the eternal kingdom. That sin had to be remitted through repentance to regain possession of the heavenly kingdom.

God saw the condition and motive of the heart of man and how crooked it had become because of the sin. Mankind was chased out of the garden of Eden and every effort to regain the access to the tree of life was barred by a cherubim and a flaming sword put by God, flashing back and forth to guard the way to the tree of life.

Mankind could not regain the lost inheritance without true repentance for the forgiveness of sin. God had to put another pathway in place to appeal to the heart of man to embrace the kingdom. If Adam had not sinned, would that new path had come into existence? Probably not in the way it did. I believe that salvation of mankind by Christ's going to the cross may not have been required in the manner it later happened. Perhaps God would have probably utilized other ways to usher mankind into the spiritual kingdom set apart for him. This may have involved the establishment of a long-lasting relationship and fellowship with mankind until the fullness of time when he would possess the inheritance.

So God now had to blend the original plan he had with mankind together with a remedy for Adam's sin. I suppose this is then why God resorted to the use of other means for mankind to get a better understanding of the kingdom. Faith says believing is seeing, but God had to provide multiple models with tangible objects in order for mankind to be able to believe. If only that helped, mankind was ever seeing but never perceiving.

4

God's Sovereign Choice

After Adam was chased out from the garden of Eden, God had to implement alternative measures in order to revive and restore the hope of mankind. The man he had created had succumbed to the devil's plot and neglected the reward of eternal life by not taking heed of God's instructions. As a result, God started to choose for himself physical human figures from among mankind in every generation to carry his favor and fulfill his will. It was thought that words from fellow man would appeal to the hearts of the others. This was another chance given to mankind to align with the plan of God.

Instead of pointing mankind to a heavenly kingdom, God now decided to confer to him a tangible physical kingdom as a shadow of the heavenly kingdom. However, this was not to come on a silver platter as well. Obedience was still tested as God gave instructions and guidelines for the proper conduct of mankind and how that kingdom would be possessed. The purpose was for God to give mankind a glimpse of the future and have them feel what it means to belong and own a particular kingdom.

This is then how I presume it all unfolded. Adam had two sons; one named Cain, who enjoyed working on the soil like his father and another called Abel who loved tending the flock. The life of Cain and Abel was a lesson for Adam who was put in God's shoes by being made to enjoy the company of his children and develop a relationship of love. It was a case study given to Adam for him to visualize the predicament of his sin and maybe realize how God felt when his spirit lost eternal life as a result of sin. To a certain extent, Cain was a typology of his father Adam who worked on the ground and enjoyed the fruits of his labor. The Scriptures say,

> In the course of time Cain brought some of the fruits of the soil as an offering to the Lord. And Abel also brought an offering—fat portions from some of the firstborn of his flock. The Lord looked with favor on Abel and his offering, but on Cain and his offering he did not look with favor. So Cain was very angry, and his face was downcast. (Gen 4:3–5)

God had asked for a sacrifice from each of them and both sacrifices were meant to please God, but he accepted one and rejected the other. Maybe the quality of the offerings were different but I also believe that the condition of Cain and Abel's hearts before God had an influence on the outcome. The Scriptures say, "By faith Abel brought God a better offering than Cain did. By faith he was commended as righteous, when God spoke well of his offerings. And by faith Abel still speaks, even though he is dead" (Heb 11:4).

I believe that faith is the absolute conviction that the word of God is established upon being said. It is that certainty upon which the centurion man refused to let Jesus Christ go to his house for the healing of his servant. The Scriptures say, "The centurion replied, 'Lord, I do not deserve to have you come under my roof. But just say the word, and my servant will be healed'" (Matt 8:8).

Peter, the disciple of Jesus Christ, at one time also developed this faith when he said, "Lord, if it's you, tell me to come to you on the water" (Matt 14:28). Upon hearing the word "come" from Jesus Christ, Peter got down out of the boat and walked on the water toward him.

Faith is in the ability of the soul of a man to be obedient to the instructions and word of God. This could be the same faith that

Abel developed regarding the sacrifice. Probably there were a set of instructions given to Cain regarding the offering that was to be chosen and brought before the Lord; this may have included its quality, handling, or the manner in which the sacrifice was to be presented. If that was the case, then maybe Cain did not believe in the directions for the sacrifice and it had repercussions the same way Adams' disobedience led to sin.

In his anger, Cain killed his brother Abel. There is a record in the Scriptures that says, "Then the Lord said to Cain, 'Where is your brother Abel?' 'I don't know,' he replied. 'Am I my brother's keeper?'" (Gen 4:9). God searched for Abel in the same way he had looked out for the soul of mankind after Adam had sinned. Cain followed the path of his father Adam as his potential lack of faith and disobedience also came with pride and failure to accept any wrongdoing. This was clear from the rude response Cain gave to God. Because of that kind of arrogance, Cain was put under a curse and driven from the ground and wandered the same way Adam was chased from the garden of Eden. The ground he worked on ceased to be productive and all this happened before Adam's eyes.

I suppose this made Adam reflect and see himself in Cain at a time when he endured the pain of losing his son Abel. The grief Adam had in losing Abel was to bring to his attention the pain God had in losing the dearly loved soul of mankind as a result of sin. It was that sin which had resulted in loss and separation from eternal life, likened to death of the spirit. I believe God illustrated this to Adam by having him witness physical death and separation in the death of his son Abel. However, God left room for the soul of mankind to be able to call, seek, and find him. If God could hear and acknowledge the calling of the blood of Abel, surely he would listen to the cry of the soul of mankind reaching out to him.

The Scriptures say,

> The Lord is compassionate and gracious, slow to anger, abounding in love. He will not always accuse, nor will

he harbor his anger forever; he does not treat us as our sins deserve or repay us according to our iniquities. As a father has compassion on his children, so the Lord has compassion on those who fear him; for he knows how we are formed, he remembers that we are dust. (Ps 103:8–10, 13–14)

God spared the life of Cain because of mercy, the same mercy he had shown to his father Adam.

Further on, the word of God says, "When Adam had lived 130 years, he had a son in his own likeness, in his own image; and he named him Seth" (Gen 5:3). This is the same Adam who had been created in the image of God. This may imply that the offspring from Adam carried his image, the sinful nature with lust of the flesh. Furthermore, the Scriptures say, "Seth also had a son, and he named him Enosh. At that time people began to call on the name of the Lord" (Gen 4:26).

This was a turning point in the history of mankind as the readiness for reconciliation with God became very real and evident. God now had the obligation to reveal mysteries of his kingdom to mankind as the Scriptures say, "Call to me and I will answer you and tell you great and unsearchable things you do not know" (Jer 33:3).

In another generation God put a man called Enoch, a man who was commended for his fellowship with him which lasted for around 300 years, had great revelations, and became the first to prophesy about judgement and the eternal kingdom of God. The Scriptures say that with passage of time "Enoch walked faithfully with God; then he was no more, because God took him away" (Gen 5:24).

God again raised another man who was righteous in his generation, a man called Noah. The Scriptures say, "This is the account of Noah and his family. Noah was a righteous man, blameless among the people of his time, and he walked faithfully with God" (Gen

6:9). But during Noah's time, God was angry with mankind for their continued rebellion.

> The Lord saw how great the wickedness of the human race had become on the earth, and that every inclination of the thoughts of the human heart was only evil all the time. The Lord regretted that he had made human beings on the earth, and his heart was deeply troubled. So the Lord said, "I will wipe from the face of the earth the human race I have created—and with them the animals, the birds, and the creatures that move along the ground—for I regret that I have made them." (Gen 6:5–7)

Key to Noah's assignment was to build an ark that would survive the wrath of God and to prove that he had the ability to follow God's instructions. Noah was given the type of wood to be used, to which he did not use any substitute. All the measurements and dimensions given by God were to be followed to guarantee life for Noah, his family, and all the creatures aboard. The ark was to be built with the exact measurements for it to be the type of ark that would survive the flood—an ark with a pattern from the heavenly realms. God had to do this as he knew the hearts of man, as it is in the nature of the mortal to be disobedient to God.

As an example, when Moses led the Israelites to the promised land at some stage God provided them with food that is normally reserved for the angels, manna from heaven! Moses said to the people that none of the manna was to be kept until morning. However, some of them paid no attention to Moses; they kept part of it until morning, but it was full of maggots and began to smell. The Scriptures say that the same people were later instructed, "Six days you are to gather it, but on the seventh day, the Sabbath, there will not be any. Nevertheless, some of the people went out on the seventh day to gather it but they found none" (Exod 16:26–27). Such is the heart and inclination of the mind of man.

But Noah was obedient to God, leaving no room for excuses. It came to pass that Noah, his family, and all the creatures on board the ark survived the flood. In every other generation after Noah, God continued to show his kindness and willingness to bring mankind back on course. God then chose for himself another man called Abraham to be a champion of faith and obedience. He called Abraham and told him to leave his home and go to another place no yet known to him. Abraham believed God and that great unwavering faith was credited to him as righteousness.

Later in the life of Abraham, he was blessed with a son he had been promised and he named him Isaac. He remained steadfast on his faith to an extent of giving Isaac back to God as sign of honor and reverence.

In a number of generations from the first man Adam, the message to mankind was pivoted on the willingness of God to accept those who seek him. The Scriptures say, "For the creation was subjected to frustration, not by its own choice, but by the will of the one who subjected it, in hope that the creation itself will be liberated from its bondage to decay and brought into the freedom and glory of the children of God" (Rom 8:20–21). The minds of people were very obstinate but God's relentless effort to gather his children became more pronounced.

From Isaac came Jacob and Esau who when they were still in their mother's womb restlessly jostled each other. God had a plan to reveal himself to a nation chosen for a divine purpose. The word of God says that when their mother Rebekah enquired, "The Lord said to her, 'Two nations are in your womb, and the two people from within you will be separated; one people will be stronger than the other, and older will serve the younger'" (Gen 25:23).

From Rebekah's womb was to come a generation of people chosen by God to be the nation predestined to inherit a physical kingdom. This nation was to come through Jacob and it could be the reason why he was very determined to gain the blessing of the first born even when he was still in his mother's womb. He grasped the heel of his brother Esau, not letting go, and such was Jacob's character even in his later life. It was marked with commitment, determination, and possession. He worked for seven successive years to get a wife of his choice; a clear mind of a person who had made a decision to achieve a desired goal.

The climax of his determination was shown when he wrestled with an angel the whole night. The Scriptures say, "Then the man said, 'let me go, for it is daybreak'. But Jacob replied, 'I will not let you go unless you bless me'" (Gen 32:26). Indeed he received that blessing from God and from that time on Jacob's name was changed to Israel, because he had struggled with God and with humans and overcame. I believe this was a typology of Jesus Christ who prevailed in pleasing God and man, overcoming all the barriers. The Scriptures say, "And Jesus grew in wisdom and stature, and in favor with God and man" (Luke 2:52).

This favor of God rested on Israel as a man and nation in extraordinary ways. From one man, a pilgrimage started through a series of dynamic events that collectively showed the love and favor of God towards the people carrying the purpose and promise. Jacob's life showed the sovereign choice of God on mankind that can neither be mistaken nor disputed. The nation of Israel was chosen by God among other nations by grace and not by righteousness. The Scriptures say, "What then shall we say? Is God unjust? Not at all! For he says to Moses, I will have mercy on whom I have mercy and I will have compassion on whom I have compassion" (Rom 9:14–15).

Jacob went on to have twelve sons from whom the twelve tribes of Israel came and were the pillars of the nation chosen to have the promised inheritance of the physical kingdom. That promise was real but the hearts of mankind were not genuine.

5

The Promised Land

From Abraham and his descendants, God merged purpose with a tangible promise in order to appeal to the hearts of man. The Scriptures say,

> The Lord had said to Abram, "Go from your country, your people and your father's household to the land that I will show you. I will make you into a great nation, and I will bless you; I will make your name great, and you will be a blessing. I will bless those who bless you, and whoever curses you I will curse; and all peoples on earth will be blessed through you." (Gen 12:1–3)

The journey and life of Abraham was a true testament of faith and obedience. The Scriptures say, "And everyone who has left houses or brothers or sisters or father or mother or wife or children or fields for my sake will receive a hundred times as much and will inherit eternal life" (Matt 19:29). This was the life of Abraham; he left his household and decided to forego all the benefits and comfort of being among his kinsmen for the sake of the promise. To Abraham was the promise of a physical kingdom, to mankind is the promise of a heavenly kingdom.

The Scriptures say,

> The promises were spoken to Abraham and to his seed. Scripture does not say "and to seeds," meaning many people, but "and to your seed," meaning one person, who is Christ. There is neither Jew nor Gentile, neither slave nor free, nor is there male and female, for you are all one in Christ Jesus. If you belong to Christ, then you are Abraham's seed, and heirs according to the promise. (Gal 3:16, 28–29)

As the physical kingdom was a promise to the seed, it was a foreshadow of the promise of the eternal kingdom of God to those who receive Christ. It is from the salvation that comes through Jesus Christ that mankind can inherit this eternal life of the kingdom. The word of God says, "In other words, it is not the children by physical descent who are God's children, but it is the children of the promise who are regarded as Abraham's offspring" (Rom 9:8). And on another passage of Scripture it is written, "For those God foreknew he also predestined to be conformed to the image of his Son, that he might be the firstborn among many brothers and sisters" (Rom 8:29).

The relationship that mankind has with Christ is a direct measure of the relationship with God and it gives the birth right to the inheritance. The Scriptures say, "Now if we are children, then we are heirs—heirs of God and co-heirs with Christ, if indeed we share in his sufferings in order that we may also share in his glory" (Rom 8:17). And this is the glory of the heavenly kingdom of God.

God gave Abraham both a promise and a blessing. His descendants were going to be blessed to enjoy the privileges and rights of owning the land they had been promised. The promise of this blessing was carried through Isaac, Jacob and then the twelve sons of Jacob.

I believe the purpose of the kingdom of Israel in itself was triune in nature. The name Israel was used to refer to three significant things: the person, the nation, and the physical land. This could be a typology of the concept of the kingdom of God where the person of Jesus Christ, the church, and the eternal heavenly place of inheritance for the chosen are intertwined in the manifestation of the kingdom of God.

A few of other similarities can be drawn. While the nation of Israel was in Egypt, they were exposed to various seasons. Those included times of peace and prosperity in Goshen and also periods of hatred and slavery. This is also a characteristic and life of the church from the time of its inception to date; revered by some while persecuted by others. The church faced a lot of persecution, especially after the resurrection of Jesus Christ when those who publicly acknowledged being his followers faced death. Those who had been scattered by persecution preached the word wherever they went. Though the preaching of the gospel of Christ was impeded, it was never stopped; persecution even propelled it further.

Such was the case for the nation of Israel when they were in Egypt. The years of slavery in Egypt were tough beyond imagination. The Scriptures say, "But the more they were oppressed, the more they multiplied and spread; so the Egyptians came to dread the Israelites" (Exod 1:12).

At one time a decree was put in Egypt to make sure that every Hebrew son born was to be put to death as a suppression measure. This was an effort to slowly put the nation to extinction but that did not stop the plan of God with his people. The Scriptures say, "So God was kind to the midwives and the people increased and became even more numerous" (Exod 1:20).

It is evident from the Scriptures that there might also have been some infighting among the Israelites as well during their time in Egypt—Hebrews fighting fellow Hebrews. This is typical of the children of God even today. There is a lot of strife and fighting, to which Apostle Paul attested in many of his letters to the churches.

When the Israelites were finally delivered from the bondage in Egypt, a lack of appreciation and insubordination became rife. They had to spend forty years wandering in the desert because of their murmuring and disobedience, quickly forgetting the mighty hand of God who had rescued them from slavery. The nation of Israel envied their life in bondage and took for granted the promise of the land.

In the same way, Jesus Christ labored for all the nations to receive inheritance of eternal life of the kingdom. He went to the cross, painful as it was, shedding his blood for the redemption of mankind. It is sad to see people not taking heed of the grace of God.

Nevertheless, God remained faithful to the promise he had given to Abraham and made sure that the nation of Israel receive their inheritance of the land of Canaan. Abraham was promised a land that was already in existence but occupied by another nation that was identified as being characterized by sin and evil in the eyes of God. When God reaffirmed his promise of the land to Abraham, the Scriptures say, "In the fourth generation your descendants will come back here, for the sin of the Amorites has not yet reached its full measure" (Gen 15:16).

As it was when God said "let there be light" in a realm occupied by the power of darkness at creation, evil did not prevail but succumbed to the power of the light. The inhabitants of Canaan were to be overcome for the nation of Israel to take charge of that territory. God chose a remnant from the nation of Israel to reach the promised land of Canaan and their entry to the promised land was marked with sounds of triumph. The Scriptures say, "When the trumpets sounded, the army shouted, and at the sound of the trumpet, when the men gave a loud shout, the wall collapsed; so everyone charged straight in, and they took the city" (Josh 6:20).

So shall it be with the second coming of Jesus Christ when the chosen shall hear the loud call of the kingdom. The Scriptures say,

> For the Lord himself will come down from heaven, with a loud command, with the voice of the archangel and with the trumpet call of God, and the dead in Christ will rise first. After that, we who are still alive and are left will be caught up together with them in the clouds to meet the Lord in the air. And so we will be with the Lord forever. (1 Thess 4:16–17)

The pride and heart of the kingdom of Israel became its city, which was named Jerusalem. The significance of that city remained for generations and perhaps will remain until the coming of the heavenly city, the New Jerusalem. The same way law was a custodian for the children of Israel until grace came from Jesus Christ, so is the significance of the promised land of Israel. Perhaps it is a physical symbol to be revered as a sure sign that carries the hope of the manifestation of the eternal spiritual inheritance for the people of God.

John the disciple of Jesus Christ wrote in his revelation,

> I saw the Holy City, the new Jerusalem, coming down out of heaven from God, prepared as a bride beautifully dressed for her husband. And I heard a loud voice from the throne saying, "Look! God's dwelling place is now among the people, and he will dwell with them. They will be his people, and God himself will be with them and be their God." (Rev 21:2–4)

I believe that the land of Israel and the name given to its city, Jerusalem, serves to remind mankind that God is faithful to fulfill his promises. As real as Jerusalem is today—a tangible physical kingdom promised to Israel, so is the New Jerusalem. It is the city of the eternal kingdom of God and will surely come in the fullness of time.

When the Israelites took the promised land, they allocated and divided the land accordingly. They became the custodians of the land on behalf of God who said in the Scriptures, "The land must not be sold permanently, because the land is mine and you reside in my land as foreigners and strangers. Throughout the land that you hold as a possession, you must provide for the redemption of the land" (Lev 25:23-24).

These tribes of Israel were the pillars for the nation whose growth, strength, and prosperity was attributed to their conduct. As the kingdom of Israel was a shadow of the eternal kingdom, the Scriptures even say that the names of these twelve tribes will be written on the twelve gates of the New Jerusalem and the names of the twelve apostles of Christ on its twelve foundations. Figuratively, the foundation and the walls give an indication of the strength of a structure. And the Scriptures say, "For no one can lay any foundation other than the one already laid, which is Jesus Christ" (1 Cor 3:11). If Christ be the foundation of our faith, then the kingdom of God will certainly last forever!

Not only that, the favor of God remained on the kingdom of Israel and the land was indeed full of milk and honey. The Scriptures say that at one time one of the kings of Israel, "King Solomon was greater in riches and wisdom than all the other kings of the earth" (2 Chr 9:22). People from other nations came to bless him and Jerusalem became a symbol of wealth.

> The weight of the gold that Solomon received yearly was 666 talents, not including the revenues brought in by merchants and traders. Also all the kings of Arabia and the governors of the territories brought gold and silver to Solomon. (2 Chr 9:13-14)

That amount of gold was roughly equivalent to twenty-five tons and it was quite significant in those days. His place of residence in Jerusalem became a marvel. There is a record in the Scripture that says, "The king made silver as common in Jerusalem as stones, and cedar as plentiful as sycamore-fig trees in the foothills" (2 Chr 9:27). That was by far more than milk and honey to say the least for a kingdom in the ancient days. I would like to think that the fruitfulness and riches of the promised land was a shadow of the splendor of the eternal kingdom of God.

When John the disciple of Christ saw a revelation of the eternal kingdom, the word of God says,

> The nations will walk by its light, and the kings of the earth will bring their splendour into it. It shone with the glory of God, and its brilliance was like that of a very precious jewel, like a jasper, clear as crystal. The wall was made of jasper, and the city of pure gold, as pure as glass. The foundations of the city walls were decorated with every kind of precious stone. The first foundation was jasper, the second sapphire, the third agate, the fourth emerald, the fifth onyx, the sixth ruby, the seventh chrysolite, the eighth beryl, the ninth topaz, the tenth turquoise, the eleventh jacinth, and the twelfth amethyst. The twelve gates were twelve pearls, each gate made of a single pearl. The great street of the city was of gold, as pure as transparent glass. (Rev 21:24, 11, 18–21)

Also important to the kingdom of Israel was the temple and the ark of the covenant, which were very key in the worship of God as they housed his presence. In the revelation of the Holy City, John said, "I did not see a temple in the city, because the Lord God Almighty and the Lamb are its temple" (Rev 21:22). This could be an example of fulfillment, with aspects of the physical kingdom of Israel being but just a shadow, but the reality being the heavenly kingdom.

As much as Israel received the physical kingdom, they still did not embrace its significance, which led God to be silent for many generations between the end of the Old and New Testament in the Bible. But he was not silent forever. The Scriptures say, "For Zion's sake I will not keep silent, for Jerusalem's sake I will not remain quiet" (Isa 62:1a). This Zion could be taken to mean the kingdom of God as the Scriptures say, "But you have come to Mount Zion, to the city of the living God, the heavenly Jerusalem" (Heb 12:22a).

So it came to pass that God remembered mankind and he spoke again from among them. The use of messengers had not helped much. The model of a physical inheritance also did not make it any better. Mankind was so near to eternal life but yet so far. It was time for God to reveal the light upon which the heavenly kingdom was established and have it take a human form to give a testimony to the existence of the kingdom. What a marvel when God began to speak!

6

Kingdom of God in the Kingdom of Israel

The physical kingdom of Israel continued to exist for many generations but not without challenges. For various reasons the kingdom was divided, its people put into captivity but eventually after some time the nation was restored back into the promised land. The worship of God continued in Jerusalem. The coming of Jesus Christ had been foretold by the many prophets of God years before his birth.

The Scriptures say that Prophet Isaiah had prophesied,

> For to us a child is born, to us a son is given, and the government will be on his shoulders. And he will be called Wonderful Counselor, Mighty God, Everlasting Father, Prince of Peace. Of the greatness of his government and peace there will be no end. He will reign on David's throne and over his kingdom, establishing and upholding it with justice and righteousness from that time on and forever. The zeal of the Lord Almighty will accomplish this. (Isa 9:6–7)

It is clear from these words that the nation of Israel was being prepared for the appearance of God in human form. However, this Scripture figuratively portrayed Christ as reigning on David's throne in the physical kingdom of Israel. In the fullness of time, the kingdom of Israel was without a king and under the rule of the Roman Empire. To many people the expectation was

KINGDOM OF GOD IN THE KINGDOM OF ISRAEL

that Jesus Christ was supposed to be a person with the power to become a king and rule the nation of Israel. The notion was that Christ would somehow mobilize the Israelites with a mandate of overthrowing the Roman Empire and re-establish the sovereignty of the kingdom of Israel as it was in the days of old.

This misconception remained in the minds of many people in the nation of Israel who eagerly waited for a physical rescue, consolation, and consolidation of Israel as a sovereign kingdom. Consequently, the whole nation kept abreast of every move made by Christ from the day he was born until his ascension into heaven, making sure they do not miss witnessing the establishment of his throne.

As Jerusalem was more of the capital, many thought that the king had to establish his throne in that city and hopes were high every time Jesus Christ was in its vicinity. At one time Christ was teaching people who had gathered around him at the house of Zacchaeus who was a tax collector. The Scriptures say, "While they were listening to this, he went on to tell them a parable, because he was near Jerusalem and the people thought that the kingdom of God was going to appear at once" (Luke 19:11).

I believe Christ knew what was in their minds and had to address their mindset regarding their quest for a king. He spoke using a parable but the people still did not understand even after listening to that parable. This is evident in that not very long after that time, the word of God says they chanted slogans to him saying, "Blessed is the coming kingdom of our father David!" "Hosanna in the highest heaven!" (Mark 11:10). They were ready to see their king ascend to the throne.

I believe that it was such a time of ignorant anticipation of a physical king, which led to many to become disheartened upon Christ's death. To them he was a savior who seemed not to have saved them. Some started to doubt his authority and questioned the gospel that he preached. The hope of many diminished, only to be rekindled when he appeared to a few of his disciples after he rose from the dead. It was during that period that Scriptures say,

> After his suffering, he presented himself to them and gave many convincing proofs that he was alive. He appeared to them over a period of forty days and spoke about the kingdom of God. On one occasion, while he was eating with them, he gave them this command: "Do not leave Jerusalem, but wait for the gift my Father promised, which you have heard me speak about. For John baptized with water, but in a few days you will be baptized with the Holy Spirit." Then they gathered around him and asked him, "Lord, are you at this time going to restore the kingdom to Israel?" He said to them: "It is not for you to know the times or dates the Father has set by his own authority. But you will receive power when the Holy Spirit comes on you; and you will be my witnesses in Jerusalem, and in all Judea and Samaria, and to the ends of the earth." After he said this, he was taken up before their very eyes, and a cloud hid him from their sight. (Acts 1:3–9)

The words of Christ after he rose from the dead had a clear emphasis on the kingdom of God, much to the surprise of the disciples who could not understand why he kept speaking about that which he seemed to have failed to deliver. The disciples wondered if there was still any prospects of him being crowned king while he was still with them. But the question from the disciples was more on the timing of the establishment of the physical kingdom not the heavenly kingdom.

The final blow came upon the disciples when they suddenly saw Christ, who they hoped to be their king, taken up into heaven before their very eyes. He was engulfed by a cloud and disappeared into the sky, leaving the disciples perplexed and confused.

I believe that when the disciples returned to Jerusalem from the Mount of Olives, many questions lingered in their minds about the kingdom. Probably among the questions was the link between the kingdom and the power they would receive to become witnesses. They perhaps began to ponder on the memories of the time they had spent with Christ, his teachings, and the mandate he had given them.

At one time Christ taught his disciples about prayer and there are a couple of things that can be gleaned from the model prayer they were taught. The kingdom was mentioned twice in that prayer, perhaps to emphasize its importance. The Scriptures say,

> This, then, is how you should pray: Our Father in heaven, hallowed be your name, your kingdom come, your will be done, on earth as it is in heaven. Give us today our daily bread. And forgive us our debts, as we also have forgiven our debtors. And lead us not into temptation, but deliver us from the evil one. For yours is the kingdom, the power and the glory forever, Amen. (Matt 6:9–13)

That prayer was for the disciples but I believe it also applies to every other believer in this day and age. Key in that prayer was the request to God for his kingdom to come. There are three fundamental aspects of the kingdom that need to be understood. Since the kingdom of God points to Jesus Christ himself, the church he was going to establish, and the eternal spiritual habitation for the elect, these authorities can be viewed individually or collectively. In other words, the kingdom of God is the trifold manifestation of the power of God as seen in Christ, the church, and the eternal life to be spent with him in a place prepared in the heavenly realms. The prophets in the Scriptures mainly pointed to the coming of Christ as the coming of this kingdom, with John the Baptist being the final person to introduce the Son of God to the people.

On the other hand, when Christ was talking about the coming of the kingdom, he referred not to himself in most cases but to another manifestation of the power and glory of God. He often implied the establishment of the church to which he was going to confer the power of the kingdom through the Holy Spirit. The mandate of the church was then to proclaim the message of the kingdom by preaching the gospel of Jesus Christ with sincere hearts, with those receiving Christ taken to have received the kingdom. The message was also intended to prepare people for yet another manifestation of the kingdom—an eternal habitation for the chosen in the heavenly realms.

Before this can be further looked at closely, it is also important to establish the possible reasons why Jesus Christ referred to God as his Father as this may help define his mandate and authority as the Son.

God is omnipresent and I believe names given to him depend on where and in what form his manifest presence is encountered. When Isaiah the prophet saw the coming of Jesus Christ, he said, "For to us a child is born, to us a son is given, and the government will be on his shoulders. And he will be called Wonderful Counselor, Mighty God, Everlasting Father, Prince of Peace" (Isa 9:6).

This means that Christ was seen as Everlasting Father who was to come into the world in human form as a male child. Christ was to live on earth as the Everlasting Father and God in heaven as the Heavenly Father, with these two separate names referring to the same omnipresent God.

Throughout the Scriptures, Jesus mainly preferred to call himself "Son of Man" whereas the people around him referred to him as the "Son of God." Mary's womb was utilized by God for Christ to appear in a human form. As it is in the order of things in the physical realm, the one who begets the other becomes the father. But since no seed of man was used for Mary to conceive but the Holy Spirit, God then becomes the "Father" with Jesus Christ being the "Son." I believe Christ's sonship to God had more to do with spiritual paternity and manifest authority he carried by having come from God. The Scriptures say, "No one has ever seen God, but the one and only Son, who is himself God and is in closest relationship with the Father, has made him known" (John 1:18).

Jesus Christ had to be the "Son" in flesh for mankind to be able to gain knowledge of the "Father" who was invisible. He became the image of that invisible God.

The name "Father" also befitted the manifestation of God as a sovereign power in the heavenly realms, which is by far superior as compared to that of the "Son" in the physical realm. This means that as much as Christ was the Son, in his very nature he was God. The Scriptures say,

> In your relationships with one another, have the same mindset as Christ Jesus: Who, being in very nature God, did not consider equality with God something to be used to his own advantage; rather, he made himself nothing by taking the very nature of a servant, being made in human likeness. (Phil 2:5–7)

By calling himself the "Son of Man," Jesus Christ wanted to identify himself with any other person in the nation of Israel who was born of a woman. He lived a normal life and exhibited exploits of an ordinary man with anointing from the Father, that which we can also achieve if God enables us by his grace. To some extent, Christ wanted to appeal to the thoughts of the people in the nation of Israel who mainly regarded a son as a rightful heir to an inheritance. As the Son of Man, Christ had an inheritance that he was ready to leave with his brothers and sisters, those who believe in him. The plan was for God, through the preaching of the gospel of Jesus Christ, to make many sons who would continue the generation of those who are like Christ.

So in the fullness of time, the Spirit of God led John the Baptist into the wilderness of Judea to prepare the way for the coming of Jesus Christ. The word of God says, "In those days John the Baptist came, preaching in the wilderness of Judea and saying, 'Repent, for the kingdom of heaven has come near'" (Matt 3:1–2).

The kingdom that John was referring to was the revelation of the Son of God, Jesus Christ. In him was the light, and that light was the foundation of the kingdom. John viewed Christ as the revelation of the power and authority of the kingdom of God. When he was preaching the message of repentance and baptizing people, Christ also came to be baptized for all righteousness to be fulfilled. Though Christ had no sin, he had to be baptized to authenticate and endorse that repentance was key for the receipt of the kingdom of God.

The Scriptures say, "As soon as Jesus was baptized, he went up out of the water. At that moment heaven was opened, and he saw the Spirit of God descending like a dove and alighting on him. And a voice from heaven said, 'This is my Son, whom I love; with him I am well pleased'" (Matt 3:16–17).

These words from God were a declaration that Christ was from heaven in as much as he was seen on the outside as a man. This was a testimony and certificate of his birth and the right he carried by having come from God; the same which is bestowed on those who are born again through baptism.

The Scriptures say,

> Or don't you know that all of us who were baptized into Christ Jesus were baptized into his death? We were therefore buried with him through baptism into death in order that, just as Christ was raised from the dead through the glory of the Father, we too may live a new life. (Rom 6:3–4)

The new life for believers is the eternal life of the kingdom that Christ began to teach about. The word of God says, "From that time on Jesus began to preach, 'Repent, for the kingdom of heaven has come near'" (Matt 4:17). He continued to echo the words of John the Baptist, which is a sign of how important it was for people to grasp the message of the kingdom. That kingdom had manifested in the heavenly realms before the creation of mankind and had now come to be with people; once far, now near. The passion that Christ had for the hearts of mankind was not extinguished even though they did not recognize how privileged they were to witness the second manifestation of the kingdom physically in their time.

Although Christ had a form of a man, he was not subject to the governing rules and regulations of the kingdom of the nation of Israel. He was a government upon himself, being a king of a spiritual kingdom. The Scriptures say, "They will wage war against the Lamb, but the Lamb will triumph over them because he is Lord of lords and King of kings and with him will be his called, chosen, and faithful followers" (Rev 17:14). Thus, Christ did not even envy to be crowned a physical king in Israel as he had a higher office as the King of kings. He had not manifested in the physical realm to get honor but to redeem the lost souls of mankind.

I believe Christ was in the kingdom of Israel as an embassy for a foreign heavenly kingdom. Even in a modern day set up, the functions of a diplomatic mission include representing a particular nation, protecting its interests, and promoting friendly relations between the nation of origin and host nation. In principle, the host nation may even provide a portion of land to the foreign embassy such that the diplomatic mission would exist as a sovereign nation on that space; setting a foot on that embassy would be the same as entering the foreign nation. Christ's life was like "Heaven on Earth." He represented the heavenly kingdom that was established by him and for him, being the light from the Father who qualified mankind to share in the inheritance of the kingdom of light. In other words, Christ lived as the kingdom of God in the kingdom of Israel.

The nation of Israel was expecting to be set free from the rule and oppression of the Roman Empire but Jesus Christ came with a different form of salvation to that nation. He intended to save them and all mankind alike, not from physical bondage or oppression but from the chains of sin and death that had come on the spirit of mankind from Adam's disobedience. The Scriptures say, "But I want you to know that the Son of Man has authority on earth to forgive sins." So he said to the man, "I tell you, get up, take your mat and go home" (Mark 2:10–11). Not only had he come for the redemption of mankind but also to offer another opportunity for them to embrace eternal life of the kingdom.

Christ came as eternal life embodied in a human form that people in the nation of Israel could see and touch. He paraded the kingdom by his way of life and the message of salvation he preached became the light to the world. The belief and acceptance of that message was the acceptance of the eternal life of the kingdom.

He performed many miracles to people, even defying orders of those days by working and healing people even on a Sabbath day. The Scriptures say, "For the Son of Man is Lord of the Sabbath" (Matt 12:8). There was no law that he could not challenge as he was not subject to any of them, he had power and authority that surpassed any written code. The ministry of Jesus Christ continued to prove without doubt that he was a ruler with superior powers from another realm. When Jesus Christ calmed a storm, the Scriptures say, "The men were amazed and asked, 'What kind of man is this? Even the winds and the waves obey him!'" (Matt 8:27).

The Scriptures have a story of Jesus Christ in the region of the Gadarenes, where he met two demon-possessed men. They were so violent that no one could pass that way. But upon catching sight of Christ they said,

> "What do you want with us, Son of God?" they shouted. "Have you come here to torture us before the appointed time?" Some distance from them a large herd of pigs was feeding. The demons begged Jesus, "If you drive us out, send us into the herd of pigs." He said to them, "Go!" So they came out and went into the pigs, and the whole herd rushed down the steep bank into the lake and died in the water. (Matt 8:29–32)

This shows that Christ's authority was felt even in the spiritual realms to an extent that demons would tremble from his presence, without him even having said a word. This was a sign of the evil spirit's utmost submission to his authority. The Scriptures say, "For the kingdom of God is not a matter of talk but of power" (1 Cor 4:20) and it was such power that was inherent in Christ, the Son of God.

At one time Jesus said, "But if it is by the Spirit of God that I drive out demons, then the kingdom of God has come upon you" (Matt 12:28). His words were intended to make people aware of the fact that in him, the kingdom of God had fully manifested before them. However, people were very slow to learn, they had eyes to see but never comprehending. The word of God says,

> He told them, "The secret of the kingdom of God has been given to you." But to those on the outside everything is said in parables so that they may be ever seeing but never perceiving, and ever hearing but never understanding; otherwise they might turn and be forgiven! (Mark 4:11–12)

If only the people in Israel knew the gift of God that was among them. It was such a loss to turn a blind eye and deaf ear to that privilege. The word of God says, "Once, on being asked by the Pharisees when the kingdom of God would come, Jesus replied, 'The coming of the kingdom of God is not something that can be observed, nor will people say, "Here it is," or "There it is," because the kingdom of God is in your midst'" (Luke 17:20–21). This was somewhat a fairly clear statement. The words of Christ were an appeal for people to open their hearts and accept the message.

Unfortunately, that was not the case with Israel as a nation. They did not perceive the fullness of time, they were not sensitive to the matters of the Spirit and wandered away from the glorious opportunity that was right before them. The coming of Jesus

Christ was supposed to have made it easier for many in the nation of Israel to believe in the promises of God.

Surprisingly, the chosen nation neither believed nor received Christ. This is one of the reasons why the Scriptures say, "Therefore I tell you that the kingdom of God will be taken away from you and given to a people who will produce its fruit" (Matt 21:43). Paul the apostle alluded to that transfer of responsibility when he said in the Scriptures, "Therefore I want you to know that God's salvation has been sent to the Gentiles, and they will listen!" (Acts 28:28). This may be why the Gentiles were later entrusted with the message of the kingdom ahead of the nation of Israel.

That did not mean that Israel as a nation could never again inherit the kingdom. Apostle Paul did shed some light on that in the Scriptures, "I ask then: Did God reject his people? By no means! I am an Israelite myself, a descendant of Abraham, from the tribe of Benjamin. God did not reject his people, whom he foreknew. (Rom 11:1–2a).

Perhaps everything that happened to the nation of Israel was for a purpose so that the Scriptures may be fulfilled. The word of God says,

> And we know that in all things God works for the good of those who love him, who have been called according to his purpose. For those God foreknew he also predestined to be conformed to the image of his Son, that he might be the firstborn among many brothers and sisters. And those he predestined, he also called; those he called, he also justified; those he justified, he also glorified. (Rom 8:28–30)

God works in mysterious ways and he knows all those who are his. There was a remnant from the nation of Israel during that time who were chosen by grace. The Scriptures say,

> And if by grace, then it cannot be based on works; if it were, grace would no longer be grace. What then? What

KINGDOM OF GOD IN THE KINGDOM OF ISRAEL

> the people of Israel sought so earnestly they did not obtain. The elect among them did, but the others were hardened, as it is written: "God gave them a spirit of stupor, eyes that could not see and ears that could not hear, to this very day." Again I ask: Did they stumble so as to fall beyond recovery? Not at all! Rather, because of their transgression, salvation has come to the Gentiles to make Israel envious. But if their transgression means riches for the world, and their loss means riches for the Gentiles, how much greater riches will their full inclusion bring! For if their rejection brought reconciliation to the world, what will their acceptance be but life from the dead? (Rom 11:6–8, 11–12, 15)

The message of the kingdom was taken to the Gentiles to fulfill the Scriptures. At one time Jesus Christ said in the Scriptures, "I have other sheep that are not of this sheep pen. I must bring them also. They too will listen to my voice, and there shall be one flock and one shepherd" (John 10:16).

Israel had been chosen to be the first recipient of the kingdom and be the witness of this mystery to all nations. However, because of their unbelief, Gentiles were chosen by grace to bear that message.

However, this honor to the Gentiles was meant to be accepted with humility. The word of God says,

> If some of the branches have been broken off, and you, though a wild olive shoot, have been grafted in among the others and now share in the nourishing sap from the olive root, do not consider yourself to be superior to those other branches. If you do, consider this: You do not support the root, but the root supports you. You will say then, "Branches were broken off so that I could be grafted in." Granted. But they were broken off because of unbelief, and you stand by faith. Do not be arrogant, but tremble. For if God did not spare the natural branches, he will not spare you either. Consider therefore the kindness and sternness of God: sternness to those who fell,

but kindness to you, provided that you continue in his kindness. Otherwise, you also will be cut off. And if they do not persist in unbelief, they will be grafted in, for God is able to graft them in again. After all, if you were cut out of an olive tree that is wild by nature, and contrary to nature were grafted into a cultivated olive tree, how much more readily will these, the natural branches, be grafted into their own olive tree! (Rom 11:17-24)

God loved the nation of Israel and did not permanently turn his back on them. The Scriptures say,

> I do not want you to be ignorant of this mystery, brothers and sisters, so that you may not be conceited: Israel has experienced a hardening in part until the full number of the Gentiles has come in, and in this way all Israel will be saved. As it is written: "The deliverer will come from Zion; he will turn godlessness away from Jacob. And this is my covenant with them when I take away their sins." As far as the gospel is concerned, they are enemies for your sake; but as far as election is concerned, they are loved on account of the patriarchs, for God's gifts and his call are irrevocable. Just as you who were at one time disobedient to God have now received mercy as a result of their disobedience, so they too have now become disobedient in order that they too may now receive mercy as a result of God's mercy to you. For God has bound everyone over to disobedience so that he may have mercy on them all. (Rom 11:25-32)

So was the nature of the love of God to the people he had chosen to be a medium for the revelation of his glory. Through Jesus Christ, the door to the kingdom remained open but neglected by many. The Pharisees always looked for faults in his claims and as a result they looked for reasons to bring charges against him. Jesus was never taken aback by the efforts of his adversaries but continued to spread the good news about the kingdom. He had the chance to use his authority to resist all the attempts made by those wanting to silence him but there was greater glory in him going to the cross.

He allowed himself to be arrested, tried, and crucified for redemption of mankind. His ministry on earth as "Son of Man" was coming to an end and the time for him to go to the cross drew near.

Upon his arrest Jesus Christ said, "Am I leading a rebellion that you have come out with swords and clubs to capture me? Every day I was with you, teaching in the temple courts, and you did not arrest me. But the Scriptures must be fulfilled" (Mark 14:48–49). Perhaps this was what he meant to fulfill the Scripture, which says, "From the days of John the Baptist until now, the kingdom of heaven has been subjected to violence, and violent people have been raiding it" (Matt 11:12).

A lot of people who did not accept him celebrated the victory of his arrest and thought that death on the cross would be his end. They believed that he deserved to die because of blasphemy. They mocked and laughed at him when he actually bore the sin and nakedness of mankind by being hung on the cross. It was the sin that had come into mankind in the garden of Eden through Adam's disobedience, and the nakedness that made Adam move away from the presence of God. To the onlookers, it was embarrassing for Christ to die in such a way. However, the word of God says,

> When you were dead in your sins and in the uncircumcision of your flesh, God made you alive with Christ. He forgave us all our sins, having cancelled the charge of our legal indebtedness, which stood against us and condemned us; he has taken it away, nailing it to the cross. And having disarmed the powers and authorities, he made a public spectacle of them, triumphing over them by the cross. (Col 2:13–15)

By Christ going to the cross, mankind were restored to God and put back on course to inherit the kingdom. His death was the reign of the kingdom of God over the dominion of the darkness, not only in the spiritual realms but also in the hearts of mankind.

The objective of the revelation of God in his Son was to rescue that which he had chosen from the beginning and reaffirm his commitment to give eternal life to all those who believe. The Scriptures say, "For God was pleased to have all his fullness dwell in him, and through him to reconcile to himself all things, whether things on earth or things in heaven, by making peace through his blood, shed on the cross" (Col 1:19–20). That reconciliation comes through accepting the message of the kingdom.

Apostle Paul said in the Scriptures, "For I am not ashamed of the gospel, because it is the power of God that brings salvation to everyone who believes: first to the Jew, then to the Gentile" (Rom 1:16).

Christ rose from the dead to show the indispensable nature of the kingdom of God which lasts forever and can not be taken away even by the sting of death. That was the same kingdom he wanted those whom it was purposed to be able to attain through their life with him. Jesus Christ at one time said, "Do not be afraid, little flock, for your Father has been pleased to give you the kingdom" (Luke 12:32). It was his joy to complete the mission and give eternal life to all mankind.

Israel as a nation missed the mark by not recognizing the King they had waited for generations to come. The Scriptures say, "He came to that which was his own, but his own did not receive him. Yet to all who did receive him, to those who believed in his name, he gave the right to become children of God—children born not of natural descent, nor of human decision or a husband's will, but born of God" (John 1:11–13).

It is this flock of Christ that the power of the kingdom was later bestowed through the power of the Holy Spirit. The disciples of Jesus Christ became witnesses of that revelation of the kingdom, gave testimony of that truth, and became the first to be known as Christians.

7

The Church of the Kingdom

During the time Jesus Christ was in the nation of Israel, there were temples and synagogues that were built as places of worship. These were carefully designed, decorated, and fashioned to suit their purpose. However, the spread of the Gospel to other nations through the message of the kingdom saw the emergence of meeting places which came to be known as "churches." These buildings were shelters of various forms in which people regularly gathered for worship and teaching of the word of God. The outside and the inward adornment of such buildings brought a sense of pride and comfort to the believers who loved very much to be identified with them. And for so many years, some people mistakenly took them to be the sole definition of church.

Furthermore, some people also considered churches to be the assembly of people of various Christian denominations. The majority of the names of denominations summarize what they regard as the most important aspect in the worship of God; that which is thought to bring the believers to be in closest relationship with the Father. That perception in nomenclature brought a scramble and contest for the best choice of names with each congregation pursuing recognition as being the true church of God, regardless of doctrine and faith. This went far beyond the reason for denominations to have names purely for administrative purposes.

A closer look at the Scriptures show that the disciples did not even give themselves any name when they started preaching the Gospel. Rather, they were called Christians first at Antioch, and this referred to their way of life and conduct which resembled that of Jesus Christ. Those who honored the life of Christ took the name Christian as an honor, whereas others used it in contempt of their way of life. That way of life later came to be dubbed as "The Way" in the book of Acts of the Apostles. Those of the "The Way" were true followers of Christ who said in the Scriptures, "I am the way and the truth and the life. No one comes to the Father except through me" (John 14:6).

More often than not congregates, especially in this modern day, develop self-esteem from being identified with famous churches rather than Christian practices from a sound doctrine. Yet the word of God says, "But let the one who boasts boast about this: that they have the understanding to know me, that I am the Lord, who exercises kindness, justice, and righteousness on earth, for in these I delight, declares the LORD" (Jer 9:24). Many members of denominations do not have the knowledge of the power and glory of God and yet they boast to be part of the church.

The global sprouting of the denominations ultimately gave an impression that each denomination was a separate body of Christ. But is that the case? The word of God says, "Just as a body, though one, has many parts, but all its many parts form one body, so it is with Christ. For we were all baptized by one Spirit so as to form one body—whether Jews or Gentiles, slave or free—and we were all given the one Spirit to drink" (1 Cor 12:12–13). I believe that the mandate of Jesus Christ to his disciples was to make disciples from all nations and have them belong to one body, his church.

But since God is Spirit, the meaning of the body of Christ needs to be ascertained in defining the church. I believe the actual church has little to do with denomination names, physical meeting places, or physical human bodies in any particular assembly of believers but it is a spiritual kingdom made up of souls of believers who have been called by God. This call is different from the calling of people into ministry as in the case of pastors and other ministers of the gospel but it is a call of salvation to all mankind. The Scriptures say, "No one can come to me unless the Father who sent me draws them, and I will raise them up at the last day" (John 6:44).

Jesus Christ may be considered as the first to directly proclaim the existence of this church in the New Testament. The Scriptures say that there was a man named Andrew, who was a disciple of John the Baptist. He then later became a follower of Jesus Christ. "The first thing Andrew did was to find his brother Simon and tell him, 'We have found the Messiah' (that is, the Christ). And he brought him to Jesus. Jesus looked at him and said, 'You are Simon son of John. You will be called Cephas' (which, when translated, is Peter)" (John 1:41–42).

Simon pondered these words in his heart, perhaps did not even know how and when he was going to become Cephas. After a passage of some time, the word of God says, "When Jesus came to the region of Caesarea Philippi, he asked his disciples, "Who do people say the Son of Man is?" (Matt 16:13). Simon was there, and so was his brother Andrew who had earlier on confessed to have met the Messiah.

The Scriptures say, "They replied, 'Some say John the Baptist; others say Elijah; and still others, Jeremiah or one of the prophets.' 'But what about you?' he asked. 'Who do you say I am?'" (Matt 16:14–15). It was easier for the disciples to give the opinions of other people than their own.

The question from Jesus Christ and the answers from the disciples follow a predominantly similar sequence as an earlier event when John the Baptist was approached by the priests and Levites questioning him about his identity. These events show that many people had different thoughts about Christ and his true identity. It was quite surprising that even Andrew who had introduced Simon to Christ could not openly confess his faith. The question from Christ must have been very difficult.

Nevertheless, I believe that the moment was the fullness of time for Simon whose name, when translated, may mean to hear or listen. When Christ asked who do people say the Son of Man was, I suppose the drive for asking the question was to solicit for his physical identity. He was born of a woman and born under the law. However, the subsequent question that was directed to the chosen twelve quizzed them about his deity. Probably Simon heard the implication of that question from Christ, which made him better placed to give an answer.

"Simon Peter answered, 'You are the Messiah, the Son of the living God.' Jesus replied, 'Blessed are you, Simon son of Jonah, for this was not revealed to you by flesh and blood, but by my Father in heaven'" (Matt 16:16–17). I believe that as John the Baptist was the voice to the nation of Israel in receiving instructions from God and declaring the coming of the kingdom of God in the manifestation of Christ, so was Simon. He became the vessel of God in revealing the other dimension of the kingdom that was going to remain when Christ was no longer among them in human form.

The confession of Simon was not from hearing from his brother Andrew as his name suggested, but his spirit had gained access to the heavenly realms and received from God the message that he boldly confirmed; it was a revelation from the divine. The precedence of receiving information from God regarding the identity of Christ was set by John the Baptist. He might as well have heard from his mother Elizabeth that Mary the mother of Jesus had given birth to the Messiah as they were related. However, his personal knowledge of Christ came from the confirmation made by God to him. The Scriptures say, "And I myself did not know him, but the one who sent me to baptize with water told me, 'The man on whom you see the Spirit come down and remain is the one

THE CHURCH OF THE KINGDOM

who will baptize with the Holy Spirit.' I have seen and I testify that this is God's Chosen One" (John 1:33–34).

When Simon proclaimed that Jesus was Christ and the Son of God who is true and living, the time for him to be called Cephas had fully come. Jesus said to Simon, "And I tell you that you are Peter, and on this rock I will build my church, and the gates of Hades will not overcome it" (Matt 16:18). Among other meanings, the name Peter may be translated to also mean shifting sand, pebble, or a small rock; it may be an error though to say that the church was established on Peter.

The reference to rock in the establishment of the church may have been an illustration in the physical realm of that which had been founded in the heavenly realms. In other words, when Jesus Christ renamed Simon to Peter, it was a confirmation of a shift from the knowledge that comes from hearing by natural means as from his brother Andrew to perceiving from revelation. Figuratively, I believe the same way stones hold together to form a solid foundation and wall of the whole structure, so was the revelation of Simon. It is upon such a solid foundation of revelation from God that the church was established and permanently holds together to last forever. The revelation of God bestowed on the church was solid, extensive, and steadfast as a rock and it has been purposed to be evident in those who belong to the spiritual body of Christ. The spirit inside mankind was to be empowered by the Holy Spirit to be able to receive revelations from God pertaining to his will, purpose, and plan.

Imminently, after the declaration of the grand plan for the establishment of the church, the devil tried to make use of the same Peter who had a proven capacity to receive information from the heavenly realms. Satan spoke to him promptly with a persuasive agenda to try and impede the manifestation of the church of the kingdom. Peter took Jesus Christ aside and rebuked him about going to the cross and the Scriptures say, "Jesus turned and said to

Peter, 'Get behind me, Satan! You are a stumbling block to me; you do not have in mind the concerns of God, but merely human concerns'" (Matt 16:23). Christ realized the source of Peter's revelation that it was not from God but the evil one.

This raises great awareness even to believers today who are mostly spiritual and love to speak about the mysteries of the kingdom of God. The powers of darkness also operate from the heavenly realms and can empower people to spread heresy. The word of God says, "Watch out for false prophets. They come to you in sheep's clothing, but inwardly they are ferocious wolves" (Matt 7:15). Being able to access the heavenly realms is one thing and having an encounter with God whilst in those realms is another.

Christ was keen to shed more light to his disciples about the church he wanted to establish and he went on to say to them, "Truly I tell you, some who are standing here will not taste death before they see that the kingdom of God has come with power" (Mark 9:1). I believe that the kingdom that was being referred to was not the manifestation of the eternal place of inheritance for the chosen. This is because all those to whom these words were said have since died, and the New Jerusalem is yet to come. Therefore, I believe that these words from Christ perhaps pointed to the launch and conferral of the kingdom to the church by the coming of the Holy Spirit. Christ was now moving from being Emmanuel, that is God with us, to becoming God in us as the Holy Spirit. For Christ said to his disciples before ascending into heaven, "But you will receive power when the Holy Spirit comes on you; and you will be my witnesses in Jerusalem, and in all Judea and Samaria, and to the ends of the earth" (Acts 1:8). The coming of the Holy Spirit was the re-emergence of Christ to empower the church. Many of the disciples indeed lived to see the day of the outpouring of the Holy Spirit and power of God.

Having been endowed by the Holy Spirit, the church exhibited the third manifestation of the heavenly kingdom. The Scriptures say, "You, however, are not in the realm of the flesh but are in the realm of the Spirit, if indeed the Spirit of God lives in you. And if anyone does not have the Spirit of Christ, they do not belong to Christ" (Rom 8:9).

Indeed, since God is Spirit, those who fellowship with him do so in spirit and in truth. I believe that it is the spirit inside mankind, the image of God, which becomes a part of the spiritual body of Christ—the church. The church has the supernatural power of a superior spiritual kingdom that has authority over norms of the physical realm. It uses the authority of the name of Jesus Christ to release this power and directly identify with Christ on whom this kingdom is established. The church extends its influence by preaching the message of the kingdom.

Through revelation and inspiration from God, the words of the disciples and interpretation of Scripture exhorted many believers. Those teachings formed the true doctrine of the gospel of the kingdom—that of accepting Christ to inherit eternal life. Apostle Paul said in the Scriptures,

> I am astonished that you are so quickly deserting the one who called you to live in the grace of Christ and are turning to a different gospel—which is really no gospel at all. Evidently some people are throwing you into confusion and are trying to pervert the gospel of Christ. But even if we or an angel from heaven should preach a gospel other than the one we preached to you, let them be under God's curse! (Gal 1:6-9)

The church was established to be a kingdom for which the inner spiritual being of those who believe belong. Jesus Christ said, "I will give you the keys of the kingdom of heaven; whatever you bind on earth will be bound in heaven, and whatever you loose on earth will be loosed in heaven" (Matt 16:19). A key can be a symbol of access and as such the spirit of mankind was granted permission to become part of the kingdom. In these modern days many people take registrations, fellowships, attendance of church services, participation in church programs, and other related things to be symbols of belonging to the church. Rather, I take these to be mere affiliations to a particular assembly but it does not give any membership to the spiritual body of Christ. There could be several aspects that may be considered as the keys of the kingdom of heaven and requirements for being a member of the church.

Of primary importance is the need for mankind to believe and accept through faith that God sent his Son Jesus Christ for the salvation and redemption of the souls of mankind. The Scriptures say, "If you declare with your mouth, 'Jesus is Lord,' and believe in your heart that God raised him from the dead, you will be saved" (Rom 10:9). Salvation is a prerequisite for those who need to belong to the church of the kingdom. Unless it is by the grace and mercies of God, the souls that are not saved may not inherit the kingdom of God. A man called Nicodemus in the Bible was given a lecture by Christ regarding the aspect of being born again. The Scriptures say, "Jesus replied, 'Very truly I tell you, no one can see the kingdom of God unless they are born again'" (John 3:3).

Salvation of the soul rescues the spirit of mankind from the chains of darkness into the light of the kingdom. The concept of salvation may be seen in how God saved the firstborns of the Israelites when he slayed all the other firstborns of the Egyptians before Pharaoh had to let the children of God get their freedom. The firstborns of the Israelites were saved by the blood that was put on their doorframes, a typology of the blood of Jesus Christ that was shed on the cross for the salvation of mankind.

It is also key to note that the Israelites were later commanded by God to redeem their firstborns as they now belonged to him. This redemption step was done after a prescribed period of thirty-three days in the early days of a male child who had been consecrated. When Christ had to die in place of all mankind, he did so when he was around thirty-three years of age to fulfill eternal redemption for those who belong to God, chosen to inherit the kingdom. The

Scriptures say, "But when the set time had fully come, God sent his Son, born of a woman, born under the law, to redeem those under the law, that we might receive adoption to sonship" (Gal 4:4–5). By accepting Jesus Christ as the Lord and Savior, the path to the kingdom is granted and eternal life becomes the reward.

Equally important is the need for mankind to be baptized. The Scriptures say that in one instance, "Jesus replied, 'Very truly I tell you, no one can enter the kingdom of God unless they are born of water and the Spirit'" (John 3:5). This shows that membership of the church cuts across any barriers associated with denominations for as long as that criteria is met after receiving Christ; baptism by total immersion in water and being filled by the power of the Spirit of God.

The spirit of mankind needs to be quickened and become more active than the flesh lest one would be guided by human regulations and self-righteousness. The souls of those who need to be a part of the church would need to be led by the Holy Spirit into all righteousness, for he gives the ability to know the will of God. A person may utter many prayers, sing praises, or teach the word of God but still may not belong to the body of Christ. Jesus Christ made this clear when he said,

> Not everyone who says to me, "Lord, Lord," will enter the kingdom of heaven, but only the one who does the will of my Father who is in heaven. Many will say to me on that day, "Lord, Lord, did we not prophesy in your name and in your name drive out demons and in your name perform many miracles?" Then I will tell them plainly, "I never knew you. Away from me, you evildoers." (Matt 7:21–23)

Righteousness of God is only obtained when one is living in line with the will, plan and purpose of God. In that regard, most teachers of the law worshiped God in error during the time of Christ. What they professed did not give them access to the kingdom but rather barred them from the outside instead. The Scriptures say,

"Woe to you, teachers of the law and Pharisees, you hypocrites! You shut the door of the kingdom of heaven in people's faces. You yourselves do not enter, nor will you let those enter who are trying to" (Matt 23:13).

Many doctrines even to this day are stumbling blocks in the ways of those who may be earnestly seeking life with Christ. The Scriptures say, "For I tell you that unless your righteousness surpasses that of the Pharisees and the teachers of the law, you will certainly not enter the kingdom of heaven" (Matt 5:20). Many of the Pharisees sought to worship and please God by strict adherence of the law but neglected its fulfillment in Jesus Christ. The Scriptures say, "But now apart from the law the righteousness of God has been made known, to which the Law and the Prophets testify. This righteousness is given through faith in Jesus Christ to all who believe. There is no difference between Jew and Gentile, for all have sinned and fall short of the glory of God" (Rom 3:21–23).

The longing to belong to the church must come from a pure conscience, a genuine passion, and an open heart ready to be filled with the treasures of God. This is the true nature of children, hence the phrase "children of God" when referring to members of the church. The Scriptures say, "Truly I tell you, anyone who will not receive the kingdom of God like a little child will never enter it" (Mark 10:15). This may mean that to be a part of the church, Christ needs to be received and revered in the same way children do their earthly parents.

Jesus Christ made illustrations with children on many occasion in his ministry in an effort to enlighten his disciples about the kingdom of God. At one time the disciples turned the children away. The Scriptures say, "But Jesus called the children to him and said, 'Let the little children come to me, and do not hinder them, for the kingdom of God belongs to such as these'" (Matt 19:14). He emphasized the fact that the child-like character was essential for mankind to be able to belong to the kingdom.

The expectation was that church would have certain characteristics of children to receive the kingdom. When a child smiles it is a true sign of joy and happiness and does so with sincerity of the heart. Children entirely believe and depend on the ability of their parents without any ray of doubt. Children forgive and forget, seldom keep grudges, and embrace love and laughter in every day of their lives. The church is meant to be likewise. That exceptional nature of children is still being sought, even in this generation, being quick to learn and grow in the knowledge of God.

Members of the church of the kingdom can speak words by faith and they come to pass, as in the case of Elijah. The Scriptures say, "Now Elijah the Tishbite, from Tishbe in Gilead, said to Ahab, 'As the Lord, the God of Israel, lives, whom I serve, there will be neither dew nor rain in the next few years except at my word'" (1 Kgs 17:1). That declaration defied all the causes of rainfall. Elijah was not a head of any physical kingdom, government, or institution but made such a bold statement of faith. Every kingdom of this world that was a subject to Elijah's declaration experienced a severe drought until the day rain came down at his command after three and a half years.

The extent of the power of church is overwhelming. God purposed all prayers of the church to be powerful and effective that even nature acknowledges that power. Several times the earth shook from earthquakes that developed at the utterance of prayers and singing of songs of praise by believers. Christ's disciples performed a lot of miracles—demon possessed people were delivered, the lame walked, and dead people were raised back to life. This was all evidence of those who lived their lives in accordance to the guidelines of the kingdom. The Scriptures say, "If you remain in me and my words remain in you, ask whatever you wish, and it will be done for you" (John 15:7).

More often than not, the church is despised by many who merely look at the physical appearance of Christians and give no regard to the power of the Spirit inside them. The Scriptures say, "And God raised us up with Christ and seated us with him in the heavenly realms in Christ Jesus" (Eph 2:6). The church is established in the heavenly realms as is the kingdom of God.

Unfortunately, the perception many people have about the church may as well be coming from observing the conduct of those who masquerade as Christians and purport to be of the kingdom. They are consumed in worldly thoughts and ideas, showing a form of godliness that is rather futile. Their assemblies are guided by false doctrines, they move the boundaries of Christianity to encompass things that please their minds, and deliberately leave out aspects of sound doctrine that seem to be hard. Yet the Scriptures say, "Do not move an ancient boundary stone set up by your ancestors" (Prov 22:28). They too will receive their reward.

The church was given the power to influence the world. The Scriptures say, "He told them still another parable: 'The kingdom of heaven is like yeast that a woman took and mixed into about sixty pounds of flour until it worked all through the dough'" (Matt 13:33). The strength of yeast in affecting its surroundings is compared to the boundless power of the church. The world is meant to come to the kingdom for alternative solutions, comfort, and direction to name but a few things. As the church is a spiritual institution, the Spirit of God inside mankind should overcome all the desires and demands of the flesh in serving God. There is no room for idleness. The Scriptures say, "Jesus replied, 'No one who puts a hand to the plow and looks back is fit for service in the kingdom of God'" (Luke 9:62). The church is a kingdom for those determined to work in the field for the God of the harvest.

Amid all challenges and battles from the agents of the power of darkness, the church remains victorious that even the gates of hell will not prevail against it. The Scriptures say,

> For though we live in the world, we do not wage war as the world does. The weapons we fight with are not the

weapons of the world. On the contrary, they have divine power to demolish strongholds. We demolish arguments and every pretension that sets itself up against the knowledge of God, and we take captive every thought to make it obedient to Christ. (2 Cor 10:3-5)

I believe that the power given to the church surpasses that of any dominion both in the physical and spiritual realms. It has been given the same authority that Jesus Christ had. By virtue of being a manifestation of the kingdom, it possesses the power of words similar to that which caused a fig tree to wither up from the roots and a few loaves of bread to multiply from thanksgiving.

Even after one becomes a part of the kingdom and a member of the body of Christ, there is more to it than just rejoicing that their names are written in the book of life. Apostle Paul said in the Scriptures, "Not that I have already obtained all this, or have already arrived at my goal, but I press on to take hold of that for which Christ Jesus took hold of me" (Phil 3:12).

There must be a reward for the believers apart from citizenship to the heavenly kingdom while in this life. If the revelation of Christ in the human form and the establishment of the church was a manifestation of his kingdom and a foretaste of the divine, how great will be the final inheritance in the fullness of time?

8

Expanse of the Eternal Heavenly Kingdom

Before Jesus Christ was arrested on the night he was betrayed, he reclined on a table with his disciples for supper to give them his final words. At that stage, the disciples had already been made aware of the church that was to be established and I believe it was an opportune time for enlightenment on the other aspects pertaining to the kingdom. As his dying on the cross was a seal and fulfillment of his mission on earth, it was important for him to give further directions so that his disciples would have a full picture of what they had been called for. It is recorded in the Scriptures that Christ said to them,

> My children, I will be with you only a little longer. You will look for me, and just as I told the Jews, so I tell you now: Where I am going, you cannot come. Simon Peter asked him, "Lord, where are you going?" Jesus replied, "Where I am going, you cannot follow now, but you will follow later." (John 13:33, 36)

But where exactly was Christ going apart from going to the cross at Golgotha? The disciples were very keen to follow him wherever he went; Peter openly declared that he was ready to follow and lay down his life for him. I believe that the disciples did not know that the place that Christ was referring to was past the cross, the grave, and it was not even a physical location. His journey was not a mere expedition but a mission with a predestined purpose.

EXPANSE OF THE ETERNAL HEAVENLY KINGDOM

Seeing that his disciples were baffled and lost in the conversation, Jesus Christ said to them,

> Do not let your hearts be troubled. You believe in God; believe also in me. My Father's house has many rooms; if that were not so, would I have told you that I am going there to prepare a place for you? And if I go and prepare a place for you, I will come back and take you to be with me that you also may be where I am. You know the way to the place where I am going. (John 14:1–4)

As much as Christ had tried to give clues about his journey, the disciples were very confused. They were expected to know the way in the mission that Christ was set to embark on, but they did not even know the destination in the first place. But Christ had hinted that he was going back to the Father from where he had come.

At one time he confirmed that to Mary Magdalene when she was looking for him in the tomb after his burial. The Scriptures have a record, "Jesus said, 'Do not hold on to me, for I have not yet ascended to the Father. Go instead to my brothers and tell them, 'I am ascending to my Father and your Father, to my God and your God'" (John 20:17). Indeed about forty days later, Jesus ascended into heaven and disappeared into the clouds right in full sight of the disciples. It is from that moment that the clock for his return started ticking and never stopped to this day with the chosen eagerly awaiting to be with him forever as he had promised.

Christ assured his disciples that he was coming back for them. He was not returning for the physical form of mankind but to gather members of his spiritual body, the church. That which God breathed into the nostrils of the first man Adam to be a living being is the same he would come back to get. I believe that since the spirit of mankind is eternal in nature, when the body that came from the ground turns back to dust at death, the spirit departs to the maker in the heavenly realms. The spirit of mankind ultimately continues to live forever either in his kingdom or in a place of eternal condemnation. The Scriptures say,

> When the Son of Man comes in his glory, and all the angels with him, he will sit on his glorious throne. All the nations will be gathered before him, and he will separate the people one from another as a shepherd separates the sheep from the goats. He will put the sheep on his right and the goats on his left. Then the King will say to those on his right, "Come, you who are blessed by my Father; take your inheritance, the kingdom prepared for you since the creation of the world." (Matt 25:31–34)

The sheep will inherit the kingdom of light, that which was established in the heavenly realms before the creation of mankind. I would like to believe that inherent that same kingdom in the heavenly realms are various expanses with each one of them serving a particular purpose. This could be what Jesus Christ figuratively alluded to when he said, "My Father's house has many rooms." Taking the house to be a place of habitation, heaven is where God has his throne in the heavenly realms and the rooms may therefore refer to expanses in that same realm.

The conversation between Christ and the criminals who were crucified on his side at the cross points to that very fact. One of the criminals had the knowledge of the existence of the kingdom of God though he was considered a sinner. The Scriptures record, "Then he said, 'Jesus, remember me when you come into your kingdom.' Jesus answered him, 'Truly I tell you, today you will be with me in paradise'" (Luke 23:42–43). This may mean that when Jesus Christ breathed his last and committed his spirit to God while his body was hanging on the cross, his spirit entered into the expanse of the kingdom that the Scriptures refer to as paradise. So did the soul of the criminal who had accept him.

The other reference to an expanse of this kingdom is in the story of a poor man called Lazarus whom Christ said was taken to Abraham's bosom. This expanse of the kingdom was described in

EXPANSE OF THE ETERNAL HEAVENLY KINGDOM

the Scriptures as being a place in the heavenly realms that was separated from Hades by a great chasm. This separation reflects the same kind of separation that God did between the kingdom of the light and that of darkness in the heavenly realms at creation. Apparently, the impression from the story of Lazarus is that the souls of those in Abraham's bosom have knowledge of the activities in the physical realm but cannot participate in any of them no matter how beneficial that would be.

Does it mean our beloved ones who die believing in Christ can actually see us now? Perhaps yes, but the Scriptures say, "Never again will they have a part in anything that happens under the sun" (Eccl 9:6b). The believers when they die are said to have fallen asleep. I believe this is not only in the sense that they will be raised at some stage, but also because of the many other characteristics of being in a sleep. As in the case of a person who gets into a deep sleep, the spirit becomes active in the spiritual realms. Those awake can not perceive what would be taking place in the journey of the spirit of the one asleep. However revelations, dreams, or visons of activities happening in the physical can be given to a person who is asleep. So it appears to go in one way and not the other.

Even when God was forming a woman at creation, he made the man fall into a deep sleep. I believe there was no conversation that was done between God and Adam regarding what was going to be undertaken. But when Adam got up from sleep, he saw the woman and made a correct declaration about her origins. The Scriptures record, "The man said, 'This is now bone of my bones and flesh of my flesh; she shall be called "woman," for she was taken out of man'" (Gen 2:23). Surely the activities in the physical could be well in full view of aspects in the realms of the spirit.

So Jesus Christ said to his disciples that he was going to prepare a place in the heavenly realms, perhaps decorate and make ready one of the expanses of the kingdom to be the place for eternal rest for the chosen.

When Paul the apostle was encouraging the church at Thessalonica, he also spoke about the second coming of Jesus Christ in the company of his chosen from the heavenly realms. The Scriptures say,

> For we believe that Jesus died and rose again, and so we believe that God will bring with Jesus those who have fallen asleep in him. According to the Lord's word, we tell you that we who are still alive, who are left until the coming of the Lord, will certainly not precede those who have fallen asleep. For the Lord himself will come down from heaven, with a loud command, with the voice of the archangel and with the trumpet call of God, and the dead in Christ will rise first. After that, we who are still alive and are left will be caught up together with them in the clouds to meet the Lord in the air. And so we will be with the Lord forever. (1 Thess 4:14–17)

Regardless of whether paradise or Abraham's bosom are the same or different places, I believe that Christ could be with believers from one of these places at his coming. Each of those souls will be reunited with their own bodies at resurrection, as every bone of the righteous carries the identity of its spirit. The Scriptures say that even after death, the bones of Elisha remained with the power and anointing that caused another dead person who made contact with them to rise and come back to life.

The members of the body of Christ who will be alive at the time of Jesus Christ's second return will have their bodies transformed and will ascend to meet Christ in the air. The Scriptures say,

> There are also heavenly bodies and there are earthly bodies; but the splendor of the heavenly bodies is one kind, and the splendor of the earthly bodies is another. So will it be with the resurrection of the dead. The body that is sown is perishable, it is raised imperishable; it is sown in dishonour, it is raised in glory; it is sown in weakness, it is raised in power; it is sown a natural body, it is raised a spiritual body. (1 Cor 15:40, 42–44)

EXPANSE OF THE ETERNAL HEAVENLY KINGDOM

I believe that as the destiny of the spirit of mankind in the kingdom was already planned even before creation, so there is no way Christ and the chosen at his second coming would roam around randomly in the atmosphere. There may be residing and operating from an expanse of the kingdom already prepared for the chosen for that very purpose. And after a passage of a set period of time, judgement will be passed on to all mankind and those whose names are written in the book of life will be given their final reward; eternal life in the spiritual kingdom.

John the disciple of Christ had a revelation from God about the inheritance of the eternal dwelling place for the chosen. The Scriptures have a record that he said,

> Then I saw "a new heaven and a new earth," for the first heaven and the first earth had passed away, and there was no longer any sea. I saw the Holy City, the new Jerusalem, coming down out of heaven from God, prepared as a bride beautifully dressed for her husband. And I heard a loud voice from the throne saying, "Look! God's dwelling place is now among the people, and he will dwell with them. They will be his people, and God himself will be with them and be their God." (Rev 21:1–3)

The throne of God is in heaven, a place I consider to be the greatest of all the expanses in the heavenly realms, most sacred of all holy places that the mind can ever imagine. That will be made new and so will be the earth, but the kingdom of God established before the creation of the earth possibly remains the same. Perhaps God will no longer have his throne in heaven as an expanse separate from the kingdom. I believe that eternal life and all aspects of the New Jerusalem would have resemblance of physical life but with everlasting perfection and inexpressible excellence. Time will never be a factor in the kingdom.

The Scriptures say that the Holy City, Jerusalem, would come down out of heaven from God shining with the glory of God, and its brilliance like that of a very precious jewel, like a jasper, clear as crystal. There will be streets and avenues for normal life movements with the great street of the city being of gold, as pure as transparent glass. The word of God has a record of the revelation of John the disciple and says,

> Then the angel showed me the river of the water of life, as clear as crystal, flowing from the throne of God and of the Lamb down the middle of the great street of the city. On each side of the river stood the tree of life, bearing twelve crops of fruit, yielding its fruit every month. And the leaves of the tree are for the healing of the nations. No longer will there be any curse. The throne of God and of the Lamb will be in the city, and his servants will serve him. They will see his face, and his name will be on their foreheads. (Rev 22:1–4)

The kingdom of God becomes the ultimate expression of eternal life. There is no other greater way of being together with God than that; God having his throne in the kingdom. I believe as the Holy Spirit to the church was just a deposit guaranteeing what was to come, the final reward of the kingdom of God will bring the complete fulfillment. The full glory of God will be seen and so will be his face. The chosen will see it and still live. Perhaps stories of his origin will be shared with the chosen. Two aspects that Moses were denied to witness, the face of God and his name, will be granted to the chosen in the kingdom—what a honor!

I believe the life in Eden resembled the life that mankind would have in the eternal kingdom. There will be fellowship with God and fulfillment of all the desires of the heart of mankind, those who pleased God.

What the land of Israel is to the chosen nation, so will be the New Jerusalem to the church. It is a promise that will come to pass. The kingdom of God is indeed the heritage of mankind that was purposed for him before the creation of heavens and earth. By the death and resurrection of Jesus Christ, God reconciled mankind to himself and those who had become aliens to this kingdom were given another chance to become citizens. At the end of age, there will be a reward given by God to those who would have accepted that reconciliation. The Scriptures say, "Look, I am coming soon! My reward is with me, and I will give to each person according to what they have done" (Rev 22:12).

When John was getting the revelation of the kingdom of God, it was so vivid and God confirmed from his holy throne in heaven that all aspects of the revelation were sealed and will surely happen. The word of God says, "He who was seated on the throne said, 'I am making everything new!' Then he said, 'Write this down, for these words are trustworthy and true'" (Rev 21:5).

I am persuaded and convinced by the Scriptures that the inheritance of the kingdom of God will bring life in its fullest measure. The citizens will live with joy of the LORD all the days of their life. They will eat, drink, and commune for the pleasure of doing so. When Jesus Christ had his last supper with his disciples, he spoke about a time in the future when he will have fellowship with the chosen in the kingdom. He said, "I tell you, I will not drink from this fruit of the vine from now on until that day when I drink it new with you in my Father's kingdom" (Matt 26:29). This may mean that when Christ appears in the kingdom as the Lamb of God, he will fellowship with the chosen in a similar fashion earthly fathers recline with their children. The life will be so real that the elect may even converse and interact with the patriarchs written in the Bible. Jesus Christ said in the Scriptures, "I say to you that many will come from the east and the west, and will take their places at the feast with Abraham, Isaac, and Jacob in the kingdom of heaven" (Matt 8:11).

Contemporary challenges faced by believers do not eliminate the reality of the existence of the kingdom, such was the message of the Apostles. The word of God says, "Then they returned to Lystra, Iconium, and Antioch, strengthening the disciples and encouraging them to remain true to the faith. 'We must go through many hardships to enter the kingdom of God,' they said" (Acts 14:21b–22). This means that all the hardships the church may face today do not turn the reality of the kingdom into mere fantasy or ancient hoax. The Scriptures say, "Those who are victorious will inherit all this, and I will be their God and they will be my children" (Rev 21:7).

It is for that reason that the wise take heed of the Scriptures and hold fast to the promise of the kingdom, being fully convinced that this physical world is not an eternal home. Our Father in heaven is pleased to give us that kingdom. Mankind was created out of the abundance of God's love and grace and that kind of destiny was prepared for those who are willing to embrace eternal life.

Many people still do not believe in the gospel of the kingdom and they find it hard to understand and accept. However, it remains a personal decision of faith. The Scriptures even say that at one time many followers deserted Christ. "You do not want to leave too, do you?", Jesus asked the Twelve. Simon Peter answered him, "Lord, to whom shall we go? You have the words of eternal life. We have come to believe and to know that you are the Holy One of God" (John 6:67–69). Indeed, to who else shall mankind go even today and still find this eternal life of the kingdom?

www.ingramcontent.com/pod-product-compliance
Lightning Source LLC
Chambersburg PA
CBHW071200090426
42736CB00012B/2396